A WORLD
BEYOND
THE WORLD

David Jones

ORIGINAL WRITING

ISBN: 978-1-908024-21-3

A CIP catalogue for this book is available from the
National Library.

Published by ORIGINAL WRITING LTD., Dublin, 2011.

Printed by CAHILL PRINTERS LIMITED, Dublin.

Foreword

The present volume is one of a series of poetic journals, kept by the other since 1980. It covers the period 1988-1993, in which year the author was professed as a Premonstratensian in Ireland. Dr. James Hogg published the English verse written up till then (the Welsh was handled separately, in Wales). Being based in Salzburg, he inserted the verse written in the Carthusian period (1976-1984) in the *Analecta Cartusiana* collection, published in that city, and that written in the Trappist period (1984-1986) in the *Salzburg Studies in English and American Literature* series, as also another two volumes that followed. This would explain how the attention of one of his most promising students was drawn to the recent publications in the late eightes. Eva Mörwald decided to concentrate on this work for the purpose of her doctoral thesis, which she successfully completed, defended and published at Salzburg University, under the guidance of Dr. Hogg. She travelled to Wales to pursue the subject in greater depth and to situate it in its cultural context. The result was an impressive work of scholarship, which might bear reprinting, as it handles many issues, both literary and spiritual, with great competence.

The current volume covers, as well as a moment at Farnborough Abbey, the two-year period of academic life prior to the time of the novitiate in Ireland, including the months of study at Milltown Park, Dublin, preceding profession and a first period of studies in Rome.

INTRODUCTION

In our fast moving world where time has become a precious, rare good, where people cram as much as they can into their timetables so as to be considered important, the idea of pausing to read poetry in silence might seem unconventional and outmoded. Only few take the time to stand still and enjoy the beauty of words, the music of a gripping poem's rhythm. Of course this is all the more true for lyrical musings and meditations that focus primarily on religious experience, mirroring the stony path to spiritual fulfilment. Fr. David Jones is one of those poets that capture the readers' attention and invite them to share a precious moment in undisturbed tranquillity.

When I first came across a collection of Fr. David's verse in the late 1980s I was stirred by the enthralling spirit that radiated from the poems. Stemming from a boundless love for God, they reflect a man's spiritual journey in all its facets, from overwhelming happiness and joy when celebrating God's felt presence to appalling grief and loneliness when experiencing His absence. Here was a man with both a monastic and a poetic vocation struggling hard to combine them. Was it really possible to be a monk true to heaven and a poet true to earth? Could these two vocations be successfully united, sustaining each other in perfect symbiosis without harming one another? My interest was aroused and the question eventually triggered off a research project that was to take several years and which has had a lasting influence on me. Naturally, the question was of paramount importance to the poet-monk himself for Fr. David's pursuit of combining both vocations hardly ever met with his Superiors' approval, a fact which was to influence and shape his whole life.

From a very early age the poet's most ardent wish had been to dedicate his life to God. Born in Cardiff on 16 November 1953, Alun Idris Jones was brought up as a member of the Baptist Church but he converted to Roman Catholicism when he was 17. After taking A-levels in 1972, he stayed on at school till Easter 1973 to learn Greek. Despite his youth he already felt the strong urge to join a monastic order and he almost entered Prinknash Abbey near Gloucester, a community of Benedictines of the Primitive Observance with a reputation for austerity[1]. However, since he had been granted a scholarship he was advised to pursue a course of university studies first at the University College of Wales at Aberystwyth, taking Latin, Greek and Philosophy. His monastic journey finally began with a stay at La Grande Trappe in Normandy in 1974. After graduating in 1976 he made a retreat at the charterhouse of Sélignac near Bourg-en-Bresse and eventually entered the Carthusian Order in December that year.

It was as a Carthusian monk that Alun Idris Jones, now Frère David, began to write poetry in earnest. *The Threshold of Paradise*[2] mirrors his devotion as well as his struggles, offering glimpses of <u>an austerity une</u>qualled by any other Catholic Order.[3] Clearly,

1   Cf. Hogg, James. "Foreword". In: Jones, David. *In Perpetuum. The Poetic Journal of a Welsh Monk. Musings in a Medieval Cloister 1995-2000*. Dublin, Original Writing 2008, vi.
2   Anon. *The Threshold of Paradise. The Poetic Journal of a Welsh Novice Monk in France – Dom Edmund Gurdon. A Memoir* by James Hogg. Analecta Cartusiana 129. Salzburg 1988.
3   Cf. Schmid-Mörwald, Eva. "Introduction". In: Anon.

his monastic and poetic vocations are highly interwoven, for him the writing of poetry is a means to praise the Lord but also serves as an outlet for accumulated feelings, the poems stem from the intensity of his religious experience. However, the authorities of the Order felt that his monastic vocation clashed with his poetic vocation, or rather the desire to publish his verse, hence he was unable to make his solemn profession. Fr. David left the Order in 1984 on the expiration of his temporary vows.

After retreats at Quarr Abbey and St. Hugh's Charterhouse near Horsham, Fr. David decided to return to La Trappe and enter the Cistercian Order of the Strict Observance. The volume *A World Within the World*[4] reflects his experiences as a Trappist monk but again the Order regarded his writing of poetry as irreconcilable with a monastic vocation and thus two years later he moved on to Roscrea Abbey, a Trappist foundation in Southern Ireland before he resumed studies again, taking a graduate diploma in Primary Education at Normal College, Bangor in 1987. After visiting several religious houses in Great Britain, he rather rashly entered Farnborough in 1988, a Benedictine Abbey of Strict Observance. The musical tradition of the house had certainly been tempting and Fr. David had wanted to settle, but he was far too contemplatively oriented to blend in with the community, so he left early in 1989. His spiritual search continued and he agreed

Paradise Regained. A Welsh Novice Monk. Salzburg Studies in English Literature, Poetic Drama & Poetic Theory 146. Salzburg 1996, iv.

4   Anon. *A World Within the World. The Poetic Journal of a Welsh Novice Monk*. Salzburg Studies in English Literature, Poetic Drama & Poetic Theory 68:2. Salzburg 1988.

to take part in a project translating the Church Fathers from Latin and Greek into modern English[5]. In autumn he started a Bachelor of Divinity course at the University College in Bangor. During that period he joined groups working for the spiritual renewal in Wales. After graduating in 1991 he entered the Premonstratensian Order at Kilnacrott, Ireland. *A World Beyond the World*[6] covers the Benedictine period at Farnborough, his time as a student in North Wales and his noviciate at Kilnacrott Abbey. New subjects enter the poetry due to his presence in non-monastic surroundings as a student in Bangor, yet his happiness of having returned to a monastic community is vividly reflected in his verse. In January 1994 the Order sent him to the Angelicum in Rome to study Spirituality, which would be useful for eventual counselling work. Fr. David was about to settle when unfortunately Kilnacrott was involved in various scandals and the future of the abbey was at stake. Fr. David was allowed to stay at Mount Tabor Hermitage in the west of Ireland for a while but since he was not yet in Holy Orders the solution could once again only be temporary. And so the pilgrimage continued. As so often in the poet-monk's life providence intervened, this time in the person of Dr. James Hogg from Salzburg University, editor of Analecta Cartusiana, at whose suggestion Fr. David joined a community at Sant'Antimo near Castelnuouvo dell'Abate in Tuscany in December 1995. The community follow the Premonstratensian rule. Fr. David made his solemn profession in December 1996 and was ordained to

5   Davies, Oliver. *Promise of Good Things. The Apostolic Fathers.* Translations by Alun Idris Jones and Oliver Davies. London 1992.

6   Anon. *A World Beyond the World. A Welsh Novice Monk.* Analecta Cartusiana 129:3. Salzburg 1993.

the priesthood in Siena a year later. Soon after that he returned to the Angelicum and presented his doctoral thesis[7] in December 1998[8]. The volume *In Perpetuum: The Poetic Journal of a Welsh Monk. Musings in a Medieval Cloister* depict the period from 1995 until 2000.

In 2003 he first ventured his longing to return to the eremitical state and was told to wait a few years. His wish was granted in 2007 so that at present Fr. David is living as a hermit in Duleek, Co. Meath, Ireland where he pursues his contemplative vocation.

The present volume is the sequel to *A World within the World* and contains Fr. David's student and Erin-based novice work, with poems written between 1988and 1993. Again the poetry pays witness to a soul's spiritual journey paved with obstacles and difficulties, yet the poet never loses his belief in divine providence. We are invited to join his spiritual journey, share precious moments with a man who has placed himself completely and utterly in God's hands. Doubtless, any reader willing to pause and plunge into the verse will be able to share some of the intensity of the poet's own experience.

Eva Schmid-Mörwald

---

7   Printed as: Jones, Br. David. *An Early Witness to the Nature of the Canonical Order in the Twelfth Century. A Study in the Life and Writings of Adam Scot, with Particular Reference to his Understanding of the Rule of St. Augustine.* Analecta Cartusiana 151. Salzburg 1999.

8   Cf. Hogg, James. "Foreword". In: Jones, David. *In Perpetuum.* xi.

A WORLD
BEYOND
THE WORLD

ENCLOSED
(at St Michael's Abbey)

There is a world within the world that spins
Which turns less quickly on an axis known
But unto them that know where earth begins
To be no more. This little land we own,
Whereon henceforth the hours shall run us through,
Hems in the Paradise or Hell we choose
To make for our heart's dwelling. Only two
Need fully be, and, in their being, lose
The need for other beings – for their all
Is in their being all for one small world
Which they can likewise build – but this so small
Yet resonating echo of a word
That came again this night from where Thou art
Knows now somehow that two vast worlds here part.

28/1/88

GŴYL DDEWI
(St David's Day)

When 'neath the blows of many hardened sounds
We lie alone until their echoes die,
And grasp awhile a tone wherein abounds
A resonance once heard when passing by
This Siren that dies not, long, long ago,
When first the whiteness of this Vestal robe
Became too dazzling in e'en sparked Youth's glow
To let another flame its entrails probe –
When now again a face that shone before
A hand that, unbid, traced a line of life
From some unsummoned corner, on this shore
Of sheer Despair and utterness of strife,
Appears between the clouds and beckons, Come,
I know the warmth within the sound of Home.

A face: Dom Aldhelm, Abbot of Prinknash, who wrote an unexpected letter, read all the verse, and invited me to come and talk. (At that point it seemed that I would be going to him, but then, on the telephone, he suggested entering at their daughter-house, St Michael's Abbey.)

THE PENMON BELL
(that people are hearing at 4.30 a.m.)

There is an eye that sees through many years,
A mind that dreamed these things ere dreams began
To turn their thoughts towards a day's full fears
Of matters great, that mattered so to man
That he saw not the Sight that saw it all,
And would see for himself, lest Sight be not
As well prepared as he, who details small
Could for whole days map out and duly plot.
O! unchimed bell that nought doth pull below,
But yet, 'tis said, art heard upon a shore
That well records thy sound, thine hour doth know
(Since gentle boreal light sings as of yore),
And thy hid Ringer sees at His reveil,
Art thou a cry o'er heard from Hypnos' vale?

PARKMINSTER REVISITED

And yet I would return to this fair peace
That clings unto these stones, as to my soul.
That knowing that rememb'ring doth release,
Unfooled, holds ill the stirrings of the whole.
To be, and to be nought else but to be
And, being, to be one with all that is
Were to be well, e'en if as well I see
That 'twould not be as well as to be His.
For I perceive that to be here alone
Would this time be to be all one with One
That hath with many drawings gently shown
That He gives all when all His bidding's done,
And that a newer peace may yet be heard
When many years have listened for a word.

Y LLYFR OFFEREN
(HWN YW FY NGHORFF)

A glywir eto eiriau hen y Nef
Dros dir ein gwlad, dros fyrddau'n hir foddhad
Ar foddion Gras, ar roddion wnaed trwy lef
Yr henaidd Air ei hun – a fydd parhad
I aberth Gwaed yr oesoedd lle na fu
Ond swn y gwacter yn ein miri oll
Yn llenwi'r lle â lleisiau llawer llu,
A waeddodd waedd yr oesau ruthrai 'ngholl?
Ac a fydd dydd i'r geiriau tawel hyn
Gael lle'n fy mron, ac ar fy nhafod sain
I seinio yn yr awel nodau prin
Geirynnau byr Un dinod fu dan faen
Yn angof, er mai erof y bu Ef
Yn yngan sill neu ddwy a holltai'r Nef?

3/11
(Gŵyl y Santes Wenfrewi)

X

(ar ddiwedd ffurflenni a gorchymyn gan gyfaill)

A fu mewn dwy fer linell gymaint grym,
Neu ar fân gornel dalen gyfryw hud
A lledrith? Ac a fu erioed i ddim,
Wrth iddo orwedd dan ddiddymdra hyd
Ysgytwad bys, fyth ysgwyd feithed rhod?
A oes i ddafn, i ddylif hylif main,
Ryw syniad am a ddeil? Ac a oes nod
Fel nodyn cariad cudd a gân heb sain?
Ac wrth it, dyner forwyn, amgau lle
I'm bywyd oll mewn amlen, a oedd mwy
Na phwysau awyr iach ar seml we
Y ddeufarc brys? A deithiai hefyd drwy
Eu croesi mân ryw groeslif anferth fawr?
Ai dyma, tybed, ôl sawl unig awr

4/11

Effacé

To be – nay, nay, and nothing but to be
A being that is part of all that is –
Is all that now remains, for herein we
In lying in the Isness that is His
Are made as He had made us, not alone
A glory to an hour that waited not
Upon our act, but mightily struck down
To be a spark of glory here forgot.
Ω Μοναχέ! – to be this very thing
Wherewith thou'rt named – to be a oned of soul
That looks upon a Gazing, speaks to sing
And moves within the rhythm of the whole
Of cosmic Dance – this is this night to live
Within the ecstasy that two can give.

10/12/88
(St John Roberts, reprise d'habit)

7

A VIRGIN NEW YEAR

My heart has its own secret, and a song
Known only to one soul, the one that here
Unseen, unknown, would flee the busy throng
Of uncontainèd spirits that ill steer
The energies within that could return
To their first point, the spot whence all rays starred,
The spark of being's glowing, – could they burn
But less in burning out such forces marred.
I say, known to one soul, yet there are twain
In earthly flesh that listen to this sound
Of inward singing, for somehow again
The heart that throbs within a throb hath found
That answers to its beating, hears th'unheard,
And fondles with a pulsing of traced word.

READING

The force of Word is in its rebound call,
The silence wherein echoes all it holds.
A syllable of Sense, if let to fall
Upon a cushioned rest, no more withholds
Its germ of life. There are but rarely times
When Time may not be staggered in its flow
And made to hear its murmuring betimes
Ere it pull on and on whither we go.
We hear the sound of thumping in our ears,
For Noise holds well its audience as it makes
Each itch well-scratched; yet feel not fall the tears
Of little things, sweet things shed for our sakes
By small unhurried angels that see all
We miss as on we press without recall.

Dawn over Farnborough

As I look down upon these many lights
That shine, each one, upon a world – their own
Embedded myst'ry of sweet-dreamt delights
Now slumb'ring in a happiness unknown –
As I behold the distant flicker fade
Beneath a sanguine hue, as I look on
At what the hands of many men have made
To hold the hours of weal and woe here won,
I think again on what it is to know
The song of Earth, the knowledge of the thing
That makes the unknown known to them that go
Along this path without a song to sing –
I mean, to hear a sound that only some
Have heard in this small word that utters Home.

FRANCE, MA FRANCE!
(le jeudi qui correspond à peu près
au jeudi du départ, 23/1/86)

Ce jour m'apporte un jour de souvenirs
Trop vifs, trop brefs: un seul définitif
Eh bien renfermait tout bien à venir –
Et qui ne viendrait plus, car ce hâtif
Consentement ne sentait tout le poids
D'un mot qui rouvrait tant de mots si lourds
De sens, de contre-sens, d'effroi, de choix,
D'enfer enfin libéré par un jour.
Ô Jour! Ô jour qui poins et nous rejoins
À tes aïeux – les nôtres, tous les nôtres
Qui passent sans adieux sous un beau point
Que toi seul, tu enfermes comme apôtre
De l'ancien Destin – toi, Festin d'une heure,
Es-tu au point du Jour le point qu'il pleure?

COMMUNIO
(Giving the Chalice at High Mass)

There's presence o'er the Presence that I bear:
'Twixt lip and lip an inward world untold,
In breast on beating breast a thought all bare
To Him who enters – all that lives can hold
Is held within a corpulet so fine,
So fair, less fair, nay, ever fairly made
By Hands that bid my hand hand on Love's wine
To each new hand-caress – here, here 'tis laid:
Within the tent of flesh that Flesh and Blood
Encounters in a drop, within the veil
Of every hidden secret there is good
And evil in a little thing so frail
That it must needs return from worlds apart
And in this whisper have in One a part.

QUID CLAMABO? OMNIS CARO FŒNUM...
(As new bells are being cast)

A molten moment of Eternity
At this repeating hour herein is cast
In lambent heat whose cooled serenity
Will shape the frigid hours slow-trickling past
These windows that look down upon a world
Oft called, recalled by brazen muezzin sound
From its own noisy clamour, ever whirled
Back-forth, back-forth till hushed by rushed Fate's bound.
O passing of a whimper wherein Earth
Re-echoes her sons' cry, thou seemest all
To all that hear thy pain or hoard thy mirth,
Yet these new souls inanimate will call
Each dusk and dawn across a din too full,
There is time yet one gap from Time to pull.

Quid clamabo...: Inscription on Sélignac (clock-)bell.

YOU DO NOT FIT IN

I know not whence this comes, save that the word
Bears some familiar sound, heard in these parts
At this same season – yes, this pain was heard
Before upon this road. These little hearts
That throb awhile and draw to passing dreams
Till they can throb no more, hold many things
In their unheard soft patter, and it seems
That they were made for breaking, for the wings
Of youthful passion can be clipped too oft,
And there is fear in loving when the bliss
On agony is spent.

                  ...Yet e'en this soft
And muffled groan alone that groans amiss
Far from a listening ear, can it yet know
A joy in this great Void whither we go?

'Tis not Despair that hurts, but only Hope,
For when there is no more, no further ill
Can here be feared. 'Tis e'en a joy to grope
For light 'mid th'ash of life. But when yet still
A shimmer of a something lingers on
And on and on, not giving Hell its prize,
The fractured soul begins to leave undone
Its own titanic work, and sits and sighs
And waits upon a platform while a noise
Clouds every sense by nonsense now deranged,
And letting go of holding hangs in poise
Between a well-marked journey prearranged
By faultless thinking armed with calcule dense
And something out of Nothing that hath Sense.

27/2/89
(Crew station)

YOU'LL HAVE TO SAW ME IN TWO
(Easter Day)

There is within the shining of a child
A tingling that the frozen heart doth melt,
And in the clamber of a clamour wild
With purest joy, a something yet is felt
That this heart felt before when hugeness small
Filled its full world with thrills enough awhile
For these our seraph hours. We call and call
At our meridian as at our dawn's smile,
But little could you know, my little jewels,
What your own calling, tugging, wanting, all,
Did call upon to give – what mighty fuels
From need to need yet flow, what pulls recall
Of pullings from afar: from whence you came –
From whence you could yet come, the same, the same.

in two: "Ah! no. You're mine!..."
dawn: Donna, 9, and Dawn, 8.

ANGE

Ce vide qui attend attend si bien
Qu'un rien de rien du tout peut tout refaire,
Peut lui complaire, car combler un rien
N'est pas si dur, si difficile à faire.
Ô! pauvreté, Ô! dernier abîme,
Qui montres mon visage à qui le porte,
J'ai su, ici j'ai su ce mot intime
Que seul ton grand écho ici rapporte.
Ô Jésus, je T'ai cherché, je T'ai pris
Entre mes mains à l'heure de l'extase
En jouet, petit jouet mal compris,
Mal aimé, car de ce grand jeu la base
Est aujourd'hui rencontrée, montrée, vue,
Et ce soir sachant rien enfin j'ai su.

3/4
(feast of Annunciation, after
a mysterious telephone invitation)

RHIW GOCH
(man geni San John Roberts)

Ni fu na gwynt na gwacter fel y rhain
A'm hamgylchyna heno ar y bryn
Lle bu i draed a droediodd ̇gynt y maen
A wêl fy llygaid prudd, barhau fel hyn
I ddal am orig fer i ddal y byd
Sydd yn y corffyn hwn a'n deil ni oll –
Beth ddwedaf? – John! – dy freuddwyd di i gyd
A nythodd yn y fan, lle'r wyf yngholl.
Ar goll! Ar goll! Colledig yw'r un oes
A deithiodd drwof, heibio'r hyn o ddydd
A wawriodd draw, dan wenu, cyn y troes
Ei wên yn wg, yn arswyd am a fydd
Yn teithio heibio yn y fan –
Heb adael, yntau, ond chwa'n breuddwyd wan.

16/4
(gyda'r Tad Ryan)

LAST NIGHT AT TALACRE

Beginnings have an ending here on earth,
For that we can begin to cease to will;
And yet to will and not to hear the mirth
Heard from afar, is but twice o'er to thrill
At passing wind, that shall ne'er blow again,
But only be deep-felt whence it hath gone.
O emptiness! Was't p'haps to this last pain
That much, much swelling grew? Is my deed done?
And Thou, full might of Fulness, dost Thou here
Await upon the staff of æons long
For one to offer one last limb: an ear
To listen to the beauty of Thy song?
O thing! O thing, contrived not upon earth,
Thou hast a name, where ancient notes have birth.

18/6

Ending: End of the Benedictine Office, which Dom Basil, former
Prior of Farnborough, had maintained with me after the departure
of the nuns to Chester, in the hope of initiating a male foundation.

Ar lan y Fenai
(A thrwy'r cymylau gwelaf
O bob rhyw wlad yr harddaf,
Oherwydd hon yw 'ngwlad fy hun...)

Nid oes fan yma siant nac adlais mwyn
Hen nodau'r Nef, na llef y cewri fu –
Ac eto sy' – yn llefain er dy fwyn
Yn anial gonglau'r byd, ac nid oes llu
O frodyr nac o dadau yma'n dod
I godi 'nghân o'r dyfnder atat mwy.
Nid oes fan yma ond cyfarwydd nod
Y pethau fu, y pethau cu i'm clwy'.
Cans yma yn y gwacter y mae lle
I fod yn unig yn y dorf ddi-hid
Am fanion mawr ffolineb campwyr Ne'
A draetha aml ras ag acen llid,
Ac oedi ar un gongl fach o'r byd
Heb neb, heb ddim, ond Rhywbeth sydd o hyd.

28/4

PRINTEMPS

La voie qui nous amène en ce grand lieu
Qu'un jour d'antan on appelait le Monde
M'a été tracée par un ciel si vieux
Qu'un monde ou deux vus dans l'idée profonde
De sa Pensée, ne semblaient pas, je pense,
Si loin de ce fin centre qui les tient.
Ce vide où je me trouve sans défense
Contient peut-être un Être d'où il vient.
Je pense à ta Pensée, Ancien des Jours,
– À son vieux coin qui vit ce coin du temps:
Le vit, le revit, le revoit toujours
Posé à l'horizon d'un seul printemps. . .
Je marche seul en ce lent, lointain rêve,
N'en voyant que l'ampleur d'une heure brève.

29/4
(au bord des eaux)

PRINKNASH

Mae hiraeth ynof eto am a fu
Yn llonni 'mron yn nyddiau mebyd mwyn.
Ni allwn ddianc rhag y pethau sy'
Yn fwy na ni, na llwyr anghofio'u swyn.
Pe gallwn fynd yn ôl at wawr o hedd,
Fel arall gynt cyn honno, dros y Wlad
Lle sugnais ddidwyll laeth, lle'r yfais wledd
Pur Ras, awn yno'n ôl at dŷ fy Nhad.
O ddwyfol Dân, na fynni ddiffodd mwy
O fewn y galon yswyd gan dy rym,
I ba le'r af, 'rôl hollti hon yn ddwy
Gan ffwlbri noeth, a drodd werth oes yn ddim?
I ba le'r af i ddianc rhag y peth
A'm gwnaeth yn fethiant llwyr, o'i rym di-feth?

13/5
(yn gynnar, noswyl y Sulgwyn)

ABERYSTWYTH

This is the place where many loves were strong,
Where dreams were bright, and clear as daylight's sight.
This was the corner where our nightly song
Rose in an ancient tongue in careless flight.
This was the sea that lapped our coursing years
And heard us listen to the sages' shave.
This is the door that witnessed thy soft tears,
Forgotten truth, that stopped not at a wave.
This is the land where many, many things
Have come and gone – and yet, and yet, remain;
For even in deep sorrow some joy clings
To where it was, to where the sweetest pain
Of wanting and of waiting was first known,
Ere e'er Time's massive gaspillage was shown.

15/5

shave: French, rasoir.

LETTER FROM AMERICA
(Pecos' hope for a house in Wales)

Could this yet be? In this our little land,
In this our land, our own, our only home,
Could there again one day a something stand
Through this great storm, borne on these winds whence come
The rushing sounds that were heard here before?
Could this the land that knew it know again
The fire of Egryn that moved here of yore,
And see steel hearts remolten 'neath its pain?
O Wales, wilt thou again sing what thy youth
Knew well, knew very well how well to sing,
And will the sound of preaching bear old truth
Through electronic ears and mouths, to bring
A little of the Hope that here returns
From whence it comes, where still, I think, it burns?

Pecos: Olivetan Abbey in New Mexico wind-swept by Renewal.
The fire of Egryn: moving fiery lights, reported and seen in many
places in 1904-5.

Yr hen blant
(Penisarwaun)

Y mae i fore oes ryw wynfyd mwyn
Na wyr ei machlud bellach. Y mae rhin
Yn chwarddiad rhyddid a ddwg swyn
Rhyw awr a fu yn ôl at oriau blin.
Mae yma yn sain miri gobaith byw
Wirionedd am a fu. Ac y mae llais
Doethineb yn yr ysbryd mân. Nid yw
Ein dysg ond oes o dyrchu cornel maes.
Beth ydyw awr o dyfu ond un awr
Fel unrhyw awr, heb fawr o dyfiant hir?
Ond eto beth ond oriau sydd mor fawr
Ag i lwyr gipio wyneb oes o'n tir?
Fy mhlant, fe fuoch blant i awr a fu.
Cymerwch bwyll, rhag colli'ch wyneb cu.

25/5
(a'r Borth, 1/12)

ATTRAPÉ

Visage d'autrefois qui restes jeune
Et me regardes comme en d'autres jours
Tu le faisais, ce goût de paix, de jeûne
Que tu retiens, me tient en toi toujours,
Sans me quitter. Je sais ce que tu fus,
Ce que tu es, et peux redevenir.
Ces petits mots qu'ici, tout seul, j'ai lus
M'ont rendu à mes frères. Revenir,
Oui, revenir à l'endroit où le tout
A été joué, où l'amour a su
Qu'il était aimé – revenir à vous,
Mes frères, mes jumeaux, que j'aurais pu
Aimer de tout l'amour du mal aimé –
O joie! – Pourtant l'amour sait essaimer. . .

2/6
(after seeing the brochures of la Trappe
and writing to the Abbot)

REGRET

There is a pain of heart the heart knows not
How well to hold, withhold, lest it be known.
There is a secret that no pen will jot,
For rarely was a night by markings shown.
There is a yearning for what never can
Be giv'n again, for this one thing bears all
Away in its one coming. For to man
A moment is the place whence hours e'er call.
There is within the history of Time
Another that is writ in ink so fine
That æons pass it by and onward chime
As if no eye could read or see the shine
Of little things that mattered once a lot,
For matter of small weight was soon forgot.

ENSUITE?

When we have left this little portion here
That is our lot,
And moved, moved on from what is now so near,
And see it not,
When this same sea laps on and on and on,
Will there be aught
To show where we have gone?

A fydd ryw ddydd ryw fan ddi-nod yn ôl
Â'n nod yn rhan
O'r hyn a ddeil, i ddangos pa mor ffol
Y bu rhai gwan?
A fydd rhyw bethau mud i godi cri
I'r rhai a ddêl:
Na fyddwch fel nyni! ?

Seigneur, le jour qui baisse est oublié
Toujours, toujours;
Pourtant un jour à l'autre est relié:
Ce sont nos jours,
Où nous jouons le jeu de tous nos pères
Qui jouaient bien
À oublier leurs frères.

O Dduw yr oriau mawr, mae yma awr
Sy 'ngholl, ar goll.
Nid oes na hedd na phwrpas yma 'nawr:
Collwyd yr oll;
Oherwydd beth yn wir yw colled lwyr,
Ond colled awr
A'n gwnaeth hyd byth yn hwyr?

And yet is there a thing beyond this night
That we call day?
Is there beyond this sea a little light
Not burnt away,
But to be kindled yet, to burn, to burn
Where once it glowed,
Awaiting a return?

8/6
(contemplant l'île d'Anglesey,
où il est question de fonder)

(On Lux Benigna)

29

GAIR

Mewn hedd y galwaf arnoch,
Mewn hedd y dof i'ch plith.
Nid sain sy'n swn fy ngeiriau;
Nid oes ond murmur main:
Gwrandewch.

Mewn hedd y mae eich gofal,
Mewn hedd mae dwyn eich pwn;
A hon yw nod fy ffrindiau,
Fy rhodd, a'm holaf rodd
Am byth.

A phan ddêl diwedd dyddiau,
Pan ddychwel hun yr oes,
Ni fydd nac ofn nac angau;
Ni fydd ond un peth mwy:
Fy hedd.

22/6
(Ar *Be still*)

35

A half of what we have we have no more
When we have held it once. There is a groove
In which we turn as we have turned before
So slowly on as though made not to move,
But only here to turn, and here remain.
But further by a little we are pushed
As our one song is sung, and we regain
The centre of it all where all is hushed.
There was a time when time seemed long enough
To hold a life or two, to hold a dream
In poise, until a passage somewhat rough
Were passed, as on we moved towards its gleam.
But now I know a time when time begins
To say, Dream well. But choose, for now it spins.

YN ÔL I BENDREF

A welaf eto'r fan y bu i ni
Gyfarfod gynt dan wenau ieuanc ras?
A glywaf hen, hen wres dy eiriau di
Yn tawel dreiddio, fel yn oriau'r clas,
Y fron lle'r wyt o hyd? A oes rhyw awr
Lle nad yw'r eitha'n bod? Ac a oes lle
Sy'n cynnal ar y ddaear yma 'nawr
Ryw fymryn mwy o oriau maith y Ne'?
Ai dyma'r fan lle bu i lawer un
Gyfarfod â'r cyffyrddiad nad yw'n bod
Ond yn yr hyn nas teimlir? Hedd ei hun
Oedd y cyffyrddiad mawr, a dyma nod
Y babell lle bu rhywrai yn gwneud nyth,
Yn dechrau canu cân a genid byth.

16/7

A COSTLY WORD

A word when never said is never known,
And when a thought moves not the air, the mind
Hears not its neighbour's thinking. Rarely shown
Were views of thought to eyes of human kind,
E'en though the souls of some saw more than sight.
But this small word here spoken, little man,
With rapid thought, and with more rapid flight,
Fled from thy breast and left thee pale and wan.
It did not know that love had not a place
In this new world that others had devised.
How can he be my enemy, whose face
I never saw? said youth when well advised
By years to stab and stab and hurt and kill,
And not to die till death had had its fill.

4/8
(feast of the clairvoyant Curé d'Ars)

A costly word...: Lines written after hearing of the way a soldier of
twenty-two was bound to a cannon and shot.

Y GOSBER AR YNYS TYSILIO

Bu yma rywrai gynt yn gwneuthur hyn,
Ac eraill gyda machlud llawer dydd
A fu cyn hwn, dan orchudd cwmwl gwyn
Y tystion lu, yn cadw oedfa ffydd,
Cyn mynd, fel ninnau, ar eu taith i'w plith.
Mae yma olion gweddi, olion bod
Yn nes i'r Bod a roddodd yma wlith
Ei gynnar law, dan hen bellennig rod.
Mae yn y fangre hon ryw aros maith
Am wawr i fod, a chofio gwawriau fu
Yn troi bob un yn fachlud wedi'r daith
I'r gorffwysfannau hyn, lle'r erys su
O ryw hen firi glywyd unwaith ddoe
Ac echdoe cynt, lle cym'rai eraill hoe.

GWREICHION

Nid oedd na llewych na thywyllwch maith
Yng ngwacter hen yr oesoedd cyn eu creu.
Ni chrwydrai'r un pelydryn ar ei daith
Drwy grombil Bod cyn i ronynnau weu
Rhyw lwybr iddo ar gadwyni brau
Y pethau bach. Ni chlywyd chwaith na llef
Nac adlef y diddymdra ddaliai 'nghau
Ym mhellaf gyrion ei ddychymyg Ef.
Ond yr oedd cyffro draw tu draw i'r byd
Na feiddiai fod gan nad oedd iddo le
Yng nghwmni'r Un di-gwmni fu o hyd
Yn gweld o bell hen freuddwyd hen y Ne'.
A'r cyffro ydoedd ronyn bach o fod,
Gwreichionyn pob gwreichionyn oedd i ddod.

Yr oedd ym machlud yr amseroedd mud
Ryw droi, ryw ffoi.
Meddyliau Un feddyliau oesoedd byd
A'u gweld yn troi
Ar orwel pella'r eangderau syn,
A deimlai wres
Yr anferth wreichion hyn.

Ym mynwes Un yr oedd mwynderau 'nghudd
Dros lawer oes.
Ym mynwes dau mwynderau llawer dydd,
Nos Hwn a'u rhoes.
A gwelodd fod gwreichonyn yn y ddau
Yn ffrwydrad pur,
Ond iddo ei ryddhau.

Rhyddhau, rhyddhau'r Rhyddhad, yr eithaf oll,
A'i alw'n ôl,
A gadael dau yn rhydd i fynd yngholl
Drwy orig ffôl –
Ai call yw gadael grym gwreichionyn mân
I danio rhod
Tragwyddol uffern dân?

Y mae i ddechrau bod orfoledd poen
Ym meddwl Un all feddwl oriau hir
Cyn bod nac awr nac eiliad. Munud hoen
A welir yng ngolygfa faith y Gwir
Yn rhan o'r hyn na dderfydd gyda hon.
Ni dderfydd awr mor gyflym ag y daw,
Ac yng nghraff glustiau Hwn gall eiliad lon
Fonllefain drwy'r aeonau yn ddi-daw.
A oedodd Amser cyn rhoi cyntaf dro
Ar hen beiriannau mud y dawel rod?
Wrth weld uwch crud yr oes tu draw i'r gro,
A oedd petrustod yng ngwreichionyn Bod? –
"Hyn, hyn a wnaf o'm tanio. Dof yn ôl
Ryw ddydd â rhodd dy uffern wen i'th gôl."

"Ai bod ynteu nid bod yw'r mwyaf mawr?"
Medd saer y sêr;
"Y mae o fewn fy ngallu i greu awr
Dragwyddol bêr,
Na dderfydd, gan na dderfydd oriau mwy
Yn hyn o rod
A greaf erddynt hwy."

"Gwreichionyn wyf, ond os fy nhanio wnei,
Bydd lleufer hir,
A'r lleufer hwn ym machlud byd fe'i cei
Yn llosgi'r tir
A dynnaist o'r distawrwydd lle na fu
Ond gosteg faith
Ein hen gyfarwydd su."

"Cei gynnau'r hyn a fynni: d'egni brau
Yw f'eithaf nerth.
Dos, teithia oesoedd byd; cei di barhau
Yn d'allu certh
I ddwyn o law'r Dihenydd ergyd gudd
Y bys fu'n creu
Y nos lle byddi'n ddydd."

Mae sôn am un, am ddau, am dri, am fwy,
A glywodd ergyd hwn, a'i hoffodd ef,
A'i hoffodd eilwaith, a than wefr ei glwy',
A lynodd ynddo, dan ei alw'n nef.
Mae sôn am rywrai a fu'n cerdded rhawd
Yr hen rodfeydd a rodiwyd lawer gwaith,
Yn oedi ar y dibyn lle bu ffawd
Yn gwthio rhai cyn hwy, i'r gwacter maith.
Mae yma ryw betrustod anferth fawr
Rhwng pethau hoff a phethau cudd i ddod.
Deneued ffin, y ffin rhwng awr ac awr,
Y naill yn bod, a'r llall efallai'n bod!
Bu diffodd lawer gwaith wreichionyn oes
Heb boen, ond nid heb ofn rhyw ddyfnach loes.

Ymlaen, ymlaen i'r eiliad lle mae hoe
Am ennyd faith
Yr â pob heddiw fel yr aeth pob doe
Cyn dechrau taith
Yr un gwreichionyn bach a ddaeth yn rhydd
O'r dawel nos
A deimlodd lif y dydd.

Ymlaen, ymlaen i'r eithaf lle nad oes
Na mwy, na llai
Nag a fu eisoes yn eiliadau'r oes
Sy'n awr ar drai –
Ymlaen i'r fan lle nad oes troi yn ôl,
Ond cofio hir
Yr eiliad eiliad ffôl.

Oes rhyw ddyheu am ddiffodd hyn o fyd
A ddaeth, a aeth –
Heb fynd ychwaith, ond mynnu bod o hyd
Yn waeth, yn waeth?
Oes tanwydd yn yr enaid nad yw'n bod
Ond yn ei ffoi
Rhag gweld yr oriau'n dod?

"Gwreichionyn oeddwn yn nyfnderoedd bod,
A chefais gymar gwan yn gymar taith
Drwy ryfedd fyd yn ôl i'r bellaf rod
Lle'r af a lle'm henynnir gan ei waith."
"Ond corffyn o ronynnau llai na'r lluwch
A wnaed o ddim, a wnaed yn ddim – ond hyn
Y medrwn fod: dy nod, dy wefr sydd uwch.
Dos; digon im gysgodion hoff y Glyn."
"Fe af i'r fan lle'r af yn rhan o'r oll
Yr wyt yn rhan ohoni: crwydro wnaf
Ymhlith y gwreichion hynny sydd yngholl
Drwy aeaf yr aeonau, heb eu haf."
Y mae mewn eiliad lawer hir ffarwèl,
Ac yn y mymryn swn mae seiniau'n hel.

Mud ydyw'r cnawd heb freuddwyd yn y byd,
Heb olau dydd,
A mud yw'r cof sy'n cofio'r gwres i gyd
Fu'n llosgi 'nghudd.
Mud ydyw'r bedd sy'n dweud ychydig iawn
Am awr neu ddwy
A fu i rywrai'n llawn.

Ond beth yw'r maith fudandod wedi hyn,
Tu draw, tu draw?
Y llygaid cau sy'n agor acw'n syn,
Beth yw eu braw?
A'r hyn a losgodd yn y galon brudd –
Heb waed, heb gnawd,
A deimla'i gwefrau cudd?

"Mae yma ofn, mae yma boen rhy ddofn
I'r galon waed.
A'm taniodd i, a'm taniodd yn ddi-ofn:
At hyn y'm gwnaed –
I fod yn nawns hen wreichion oesoedd byd,
Yn rhan, un rhan,
O'r ynni ddeil o hyd."

A phan na fydd ond heddwch uwch y gro
A chof ac atgof wedi colli'u grym,
A fydd yr hen wreichionyn yn ei dro
Yn dal i deimlo ysfa'r Atgof llym
Nad yw'n lleihau, ond yn parhau o hyd,
O hyd, o hyd, hyd ddiwedd hydoedd hir
Na fyddant ond yn dechrau – a fydd byd
Yn dal i ddefro at yr hunllef wir?
Pan ddaw gwreichionyn oes at wreichion hen
Y cam-ergydion fu, a fydd rhyw wres
O'r anferth gyd-dristáu? Ac a fydd gwên
Fel gwên Rhesymeg gynt i'w gweld drwy des
Y sicrwydd fod ansicrwydd ond yn siŵr
O arwain eto dorf at fröydd stŵr?

Ond distaw ydyw man yr olaf sain,
A mwyn yw tôn
Yr emyn a'r hyfrytlais peraidd, main
Yn nhemlau'r Iôn,
Lle'r eir yn ôl i'r oriau nad ŷnt mwy
Ond dim, ond dim,
I'r un a'u llosgodd hwy.

Y mae i hoffaf anwes dynol-ryw
Ei wefr, ei wau,
Ac yn un eiliad bod mae bythol fyw,
Na all wanhau.
Mae gwreichion yng nghyffyrddiad cnawd a chnawd,
Ond wyla'r sêr
Dros gwys cynifer rhawd.

"Ni elli 'niffodd i; ni all dy lef
Fy newid chwaith.
Ceu greu man ar y ddaear imi'n nef
Â'th beraidd iaith,
Ond yma nid oes golau ond y fflam
A daniodd nos,
Heb wybod maint y cam."

Nid oedd na llewych na thywyllwch maith
Yng ngwacter hen yr oesoedd cyn eu creu.
Ond daeth pelydryn ar bererin daith
O ddyfnder yr ehangder lle bu gweu
A phlethu achos achos achos bod,
A bu wreichionyn yn y pethau mân
Fu'n troi a throi, a droes ar unig rod,
Gan ganu yn ei dro ei unig gân.
Yn troi o hyd mae gwreichion Bod tu draw
I'r oriau hyn, ac yno y mae un
A drodd am orig fer, heb frys, heb fraw,
Ond heb lwyr orffwys chwaith mewn diwair hun.
Mae yno fflam yn llosgi dan y fron,
Ac ni all llif yr oesoedd ddiffodd hon.

Awst, 1989

Ymwelydd Neifion

Ymlaen, ymlaen i'r maith ymylon pell
Tu draw i'r ymyl eithaf nad yw'n bod
Ond yn nyfnderoedd crebwyll pitw gell
Ymennydd y dynionach sydd â'u nod
Ar ben y daith – ymlaen i'r oesoedd hir
Nad ydynt ond yn dechrau, eto 'mlaen
Yfory ac yfory, lle mae'r gwir
Yfory'n aros, fel pob Doe o'r blaen...
Ymlaen yr ei, fân declyn, ar dy daith
Ar gledrau'r rhod, heb orsaf ac heb nawdd
Ond cyfeillgarwch hen y pethau maith
Fu'n troi ers tro – yn troi, a'n troi yn hawdd,
Cans ond y ddoe ddiwethaf y bu Un
Yn cael rhyw syniad yn nyfnderoedd hun.

CÂN RYNGWLADOL Y FFOCOLARE

Os ceri, mor ddedwydd fyddi di;
Os gweni, dewyddwch fydd i ni.
Rho gynnig, cei weld mai gwir yw hi –
Cei dithau ail-fyw.

BWRLWM BYW
(hunangofiant Yncl Ithel)

'Rôl cau y gyfrol hon lle'r erys oes
Rhwng clawr a chlawr, yn ddistaw ac yn groch,
A fydd cyffyrddiad mwy â'r hyn nad oes
Fyth fodd ei deimlo bellach, ond yng nghloch
Yr olaf gnul sy'n pallu yn y cof –
Y cnul sydd yn y llais sy'n dal i ddod
O blith y cloriau mudion, brau a rof
Yn ôl i'w lle, i'w trefn yn Nhrefn y rhod?
Ac a oes llais i ddeigryn na all ddweud
O ble y daeth, heb reswm yn y byd –
Ond rheswm yr un rheswm a all wneud
I ryw ronynnau lludw danio 'nghyd,
A bod yn rhyfedd fyw ym myd un bach,
Cyn mynd ar siwrnai faith heb ganu'n iach?

EVA

(and her unexpected research)

A little is a lot when there is nought,
And knowing of a knowing can mean much
Unto the lonely brain whose straying thought
Has without thinking reached a haven such
As could not have been charted or foreseen.
To know that there is meaning in the mind
That can be meant again, that ancient spleen
Can in a newer heart an echo find –
This is to know that knowledge can be heard
Beyond the walls of Time, beyond the skin
That held its ticking, word by lengthy word,
And that a long-lost beat still leaps within
An unknown little breast that cared to bear
The weight of many yesterdays stored there.

FIRST DAY OF TERM

How many souls have come and gone this way,
And grown and grown till growing was decline –
How many have once known the first-born's day,
And felt the rays of new-found youth here shine!
There is an ancient stream of years reborn
And made to flow again 'neath this great bridge
Where lingered and where smiled on some like morn
The faces where long cares traced not their ridge.
In half a century the orb will turn
Again, as it knows how, without a thought
For all the thinking that these heads will learn
To hold and hold in grey cells stretched and taut,
Intense, intent, attending to the mark,
The extra mark which burned youth's fairest spark.

2/10
(after seeing my mother's pictures
over the week-end)

ANGELET

Quelquefois quand la foi ne peut croire ni voir
Et quand l'âme ne sent que le soir de l'espoir,
Quand un jour n'est pas long, mais une heure, éternelle,
Quand l'aurore aujourd'hui n'a pas l'âme aussi belle
Qu'autrefois – autrefois quand la foi voyait tout,
Savait tout, prêchait tout, tout à tous, et partout,
Devenir ce qu'on est, c'est enfin être sûr
D'être vrai, d'être vraiment, car tout vide est pur.
Recevoir – seul ce vide peut savoir ce mot;
Oui, Carence, elle seule sait sentir le flot
Qui peut couler encor dans le cœur bien prêt,
Altéré, affamé, désireux de tous mets,
Et sait prendre sans prendre ses droits, ses grands droits,
Car la main qui est pleine referme ses doigts.

Recevoir un élan d'un cœur frais, d'un cœur plein,
Inconnu, imprévu, palpitant sous un sein
Encor plus inconnu, c'est connaître le don
Du mystère qu'enclôt ce lointain horizon
Qui nous garde.

Oui, élan, oui, rayon vierge et clair
Qui sais percer, sans forcer... Toi, force d'éclair,
Qui m'as touché sans toucher, ignorant ta grâce,
Et me vois au dedans sans regarder ma face,
Tu es là dans ta présence, absente à mes yeux,
Envoyée, rencontrée, appelée par mes vœux.
Toi, désir désiré, tu ne voulais pas faire
Ni entendre ni sentir ta voix, mais te taire,
Sans savoir, sans prévoir que penser à ceci
Était entrer dans un monde brisé ici,
Que tu venais réchauffer, étoile distante,
Par un rayon, un seul, de l'âme étincelante
Qui le guérit.

Car savoir que ce qui n'est plus
N'est pas perdu, c'est savoir que ce qui est lu
Devait, devait exister, et non son absence,
Et qu'une heure de joie refera sa présence
Quelquefois quand la foi ne peut croire ni voir
Et quand l'âme ne sent que le soir de l'espoir.

STRANGER

There is a need within the heart of Man
That hurts with gentle pleasure. There are some
Who walk on this life's ways with but one plan
To which all else must bend, unheard and dumb.
There is a throttling that cries not for grace
Among the chilled and chastened. There is fear
To say a word, to look upon a face,
To palp a pulse of life when souls are near.
And there is something in the unmet soul
That knows when there is knowing. There is heat
Within the calmed unanswered dreams that roll
'Neath many fastened eyelids that ne'er meet.
For we are what we are, e'en though it seem
That we are as we are in our esteem.

TANWYDD

(Rhoi gwersi Ffrangeg i Tania)

Fe glywodd tebyg enaid debyg iaith
Ym more oes, ym more gwyryf hoen,
Ac yn ei ateb chwim 'doedd dim yn gaeth
Yn hen gaethiwed corff: nid oedd na phoen
Nac ofn nac ing nac angau yn y gell
Lle cleddid oes, ond breuddwyd – breuddwyd hardd
Am oriau hir gwir nwyd, am gariad gwell,
Am lygad welodd Lygad yn yr Ardd.
A thi, fwyn un, fwyn fun, wrth gymryd cam
I'r hen, hen nos lle gwelwyd hunllef lu,
Tra eto'n wen, mynn ofal rhag i nam
Dy ddilyn di i'r uffern hon a fu
Yn ffwrn, yn fwrn, yn freuddwyd ryfedd iawn
A lyncodd oes ym merw un prynhawn.

SAIN TAIZÉ

Confitemini Domino, quoniam bonus.
Confitemini Domino, alleluia.

Rhoddwch foliant i'r Arglwydd, canys da ydyw.
Rhoddwch foliant i'r Arglwydd, alelwia.

Laudate, omnes gentes, laudate Dominum.
Laudate, omnes gentes, laudate Dominum.

Molwch yr Arglwydd, moliannwch Ef drwy'r byd.
Molwch yr Arglwydd, moliannwch Ef drwy'r byd.

Ubi caritas et amore,
Ubi caritas, Deus ibi est.

Lle mae cariad pur yn aros,
lle mae cariad pur, yno y mae Duw.

O –
Adoramus te, Domine.

O –
Molwn Di, addolwn Di.

Bless the Lord, my soul, and bless His Holy Name.
Bless the Lord, my soul; He leads me into life.

F'enaid, mola Ef; molianna byth dy Dduw.
F'enaid, mola Ef; fe'th geidw byth yn fyw.

Iubilate Deo, iubilate Deo! Aleluia!

Byddwch lawen ynddo, byddwch lawen ynddo! Alelwia!

Wait for the Lord: His day is near.
Wait for the Lord; keep watch, take heart.

Disgwyl wrth Dduw: ei dydd a ddaw.
Disgwyl wrth Dduw; mae Ef gerllaw.

Gloria, Gloria in excelsis Deo!
Gloria, Gloria, alleluia, alleluia!

Moliant, moliant i Dduw yn y goruchaf!
Moliant, moliant, alelwia, alelwia!

O Lord, hear my prayer! O Lord, hear my prayer!
When I call answer me.
O Lord, hear my prayer! O Lord, hear my prayer!
Come and listen to me.

O Iôr, clyw fy nghri! O Iôr, clyw fy nghri!
 Clyw fy llef yn dy nef.
O Iôr, clyw fy nghri! O Iôr, clyw fy nghri!
 Clyw ac ateb fi.

Tᴜ

There is within the magic of a name
A force made not of letters. There is more
Within two notes than any sound that came
Across a ringing sky. How oft before
Were echoes made to echo in the deep
That lies 'neath th'emptied breast, by one or two
Stray utterings? Therein the hid child's sleep
Was roused by something old he somehow knew.
There is a road within whereon hath trod
The author of a sound. There is a place
Where eye and eye can meet. Here stood unshod
The one giv'n once the Name, but ne'er the Face.
For there is all our wanting; there is all
Our waiting to be wanted by a call.

17/2

Name: Cf Exodus 3:1.

THE MERSEY SOUND

The sounds that yesterday left in the air
To wander from an hour to many more
That had to come – these sounds today are fair
Within the list'ning heart that throbbed before
At new-found magic pulsing in the groove
Where this isle spun, and on this beaten track
Past thumping feet again are felt to move
Where they moved once, for sounds can bring sounds back.
There is within our growing something old
That will be young awhile; there is a dance
That will be long in dying, for we hold
The handling of a lifetime in this chance,
This last that came our way – for we chose not
To be so young so long in youth forgot.

25/12

THANKYOU, FATHER, FOR THE SEA!
(Ynys Llanddwyn)

Upon the edge of this wide world we stood
Alone with all that mattered. Not a sound
That was not ours could mar an hour so good
That 'twill be evermore, for we had found
The light within the night where all began.
There was within the singing of the sea
That lapped the Isle of Love, a voice of Man,
The child of hours that held Eternity.
Yet in the clasping of a hand and will
There was but virgin trust: the thrust of Youth
Was in an ancient Calm contained; the thrill
Of Knowing was unknown; the only truth
Was what was left unsaid, for we knew all
In being for a while so very small.

2/1/90

DEUS, IN ADIUTORIUM...
(Penmon)

There are upon this little orb we tread
Some spots that have not moved. Their yesterday
To this, Time's latest child, by some strange thread
Is linked. Their morrow too is here today,
For there is Someone there who saw it all.
And in the singing of an ancient chant
That echoed in its home, we did recall
The early dreams that made unknown hearts pant.
For though we know not well who came this way,
We have known far too well what made them beat,
And though these standing stones can no more say
Wherefore they came to stand, they hold the heat
Of many bygone morns, and bid us too
Love well, ere this brief dream cease to be true.

AFRAID

To know, yet not to know what lies within
A soul that is so close – to touch without
The pulse of many feelings trav'lling in
The world that moves alone – to know about,
Yet not to know th'untold: this is to hold
A hand that is afraid, a hand that wills
And fears its willingness lest it unfold
Another world uncharted in its thrills.
O fairest child! O little, little girl,
Couldst thou have known what lay within one hour,
Wouldst thou have let this world thus blindly whirl
'Neath our two orbits, kept by some hid Pow'r
From one vast meeting in a little hand
That had a language stars could understand?

WILL WE BE IN A GRAVE LIKE THIS?
(Ynys Tysilio)

Within, within there is a lonely soul
That ponders 'tween the frontiers of a mind
And heart that, though unknowing, knows the whole
Of what is known to lonely human kind.
Without there is a world that moves and moves,
And pauses not to meet the man within.
The sound of many thinking voices proves
The thought that is not there where there is din.
Yet in the holding of two molten hearts
Within a ring of need, within a sound
Of wanting but a whole where there are parts,
A world within an empty world was found
Where one small soul meant some small thing to one
Who knew what many years alone had done.

YNYS ENLLI

There are within a century or two
Some moments that live on. There is an hour
Upon the roll of Time that is twice true,
And true and true again, for its own pow'r
Has lingered in the air to be reknown.
We shall live on, and hours shall pass away
As days and years were onward ever blown,
And yet perhaps, perhaps, 'twill come this way.
O fair, fair creature, mirage of the sand
Where burnt the desert hours, that thou shouldst come
Unbid from the unknown and, radiant, stand
Upon the tip of Earth, above the home
That th'eremite ne'er had, and say this word –
Is this part of a song that æons heard?

Ynys Enlli: Bardsey, seen from Penmynydd.

To be alone amid a lonely crowd
Made but of neighbouring of the estranged,
To walk unknown, unroused 'neath this great shroud
Named Anonymity... – how sadly changed
Is every human ant that creeps along
Such little frenzied paths far, far below
Our nest of Company, where there is song
About a mystery that two can know.
To be the all of one who is the all
Of one's own yearning soul – to be in need
Of being needed much – to be so small
In all the world of noise, and yet to heed
The beating of a heart, this is to be
The salvaged flotsam of Eternity.

14/1
(looking down over Caernarfon)

NEVER AGAIN, never again will you be alone

There is an isle beyond a lonely shore
Where two were one a while beyond the world.
There was a prayer to one who walked before
Between the waves that yesteryear had hurled
Their voice at Love's mad building. There was peace
Amid the wanting of two souls, and heat
Within the blast that no becalmed release
Would lose to this world's chill, for flames did meet.
Yet in the knowing of what lay behind
The fibres 'tween two lives, there was not here
The pining for what two alone can find
When not by others seen, nor was there fear
Of being watched above, for for a while
Two hearts alone, alone felt heaven smile.

17/1

(Eglwys Cwyfan)

Never again...: Reference to words read, composed on 21st March, 1984.

I THINK...

When one immobile page can move the world
That turns about the lonely soul within,
When one thick store of meaning is unfurled
In thin unfolding lines, when one great din
Of resonated Thought is made to blast
The workings of the brain that had not known
The pow'r of trav'lling yearns, there is at last
A sense in many flick'ring hours outblown.
What 'tis to know again that one is not
Without a use but to be used for all,
What 'tis to know that some things long forgot
Were picked up far away, and that a small
And narrow envelope can hold a heart,
This only years of waiting can impart.

Ar lan y môr...

The voice of joy has ever been a song,
And music ever hovered in the bliss
Of ancient times that came to linger long
On these deserted shores where ages kiss
The kiss of many heavens known before
By those who came this way. The hour is new
That is the old, old legacy of yore,
Left here for us who sing what others knew.
And though 'twas but a gentle little head
That felt the gentler touch, 'twas many years
Of having and of holding that were said
In borrowed harmony that calmed young fears
With this familiar language, where the air
Held happiness by others uttered there.

Ynys Cariad

O night of nights, who thought I'd see thy stars
Look down from yesteryear upon an hour
Allowed to be by One whose law debars
The coming of weak virgins 'neath the pow'r
Of something far too great? The day has been
That in its setting was not as its rise,
And those soft-winking witnesses have seen
An unmeant moment shatter Time's calm skies.
O little thing, that dost hold all there is
Within my wanting world, who gave thee wings
To flutter from a past that had known His,
His kiss alone, where His own Life-blood clings?
O cup of loving, we held twice this night
The pow'r that makes or mars our future quite.

25/1
(St Dwynwen)

Cup: Chalice, Mass at student chaplaincy.

What 'tis to be within and yet without
The cosmos bounded by a little head,
What 'tis to sense two angels round about
That look on as two souls unwedded wed,
What 'tis to have a hand held to the heart
That throbs with painful bliss, what 'tis to feel
The gentleness of caring heal a part
Untouched, unstroked before – this is to steal
A moment from the trickle of the years
That could have passed us by as two worlds moved
In distant orbits where Momentum steers
By force of Habit lives in lines well-grooved.
For we knew not as we took not the vow
That governed all, that blind Chance knew of Now.

When love seeks not its own but loves beyond
The will to have for one, the will to own
Alone that half of which a halved is fond;
When hearts can burn, yet burn before the Throne
That bid all burning be; when two hands join
And leave two others spread forth to the sky;
When unnamed angels nest in womb and loin
And offer little voices heard on high,
Then there is mystery within the world,
Then there are things which were not for it made,
Then there are hours which playful cherubs hurled
By accident from orbit. For none played
With this ethereal fire and came away
Without a wound that would hurt on for aye.

A SKETCH THAT UTTERS VOLUMES

There is a madness in the wayward heart
That only fondness knows. There is a waste
Of needed, numbered hours; there is a part
Of living that is nonsense in the haste
And hunt for useful matter for the brain
That must be tested soon for what it holds.
There is a massive losing of all gain
Within the yielding that one thing beholds.
But in the aching æons there are whiles
That stop the Void's long yawn, that ease the groan
Of calculated Failure. Unthought smiles
That shone a moment on this path of stone
Have had more meaning than vast well-meant hours
That in the name of Love drained all love's pow'rs.

As if...

O mystery of ages in the night,
O bliss of sweet surrender that knows not,
Cares not whither can lead the holding tight
Of all the yearns of two in one fast knot
That will not be unbound – O ecstasy
Of having no more fear to be aglow
In one primæval flame that bid all be,
– This is to know what knowing beings know.
O little word that came from one small breast
That could here hold no more, O little cry
That came from somewhere deep, what did thee wrest
From thy long silent sleep? Why this night? Why
Did wanting turn to needing, needing all
To be surrendered in a sigh so small?

7/2
(Llanddwyn)

WE'RE MAKING A YESTERDAY...

When on and on the ancient sea still roars,
Where will we be?
When o'er this hill, this isle, the Ruah soars,
What destiny
Will then have swept us off, will then have been
Our part, our lot,
When we are no more seen?

When there are waves and waves again to roll
O'er this our isle,
Will there be other feet this way to stroll
Where once a smile,
That lit the universe beneath its beam,
Shone all alone
Where two shared one same gleam?

When there are winds that travel on their way
Into the past,
Will there be something of this yesterday
In th'hours that last
Within the tingling of the air that held
A molten bliss
That hours to hours did weld?
When there is nothing of this day that was
The fullest Now
Of two who paused to feel a moment as
It cast its glow,
Will there then be no part, nor part of part
Of this our share
Of Joy left to impart?

And when we are no more, my little child,
And others come
Upon this path we trod one winter wild
As we came home
To this our long-forgotten part of us,
Will some one say,
Two others once did thus.?

9/2

(Penmon)

(On melody composed for it)

ST VALENTINE'S DAY ON LLANDDWYN

How empty would the world have been,
Had one soul not been there!
What hours no day would e'er have seen,
Had paths collided ne'er!

What would have been, had we been not
Awhile on one same shore?
Would unheard hearts with yearns forgot
Have murmured as before?

Would unknown thoughts have turned and turned
In orbits ne'er to meet,
And would two worlds of need long spurned
Have spun on all complete?

And had the two that now were one
Glimpsed this day from afar,
Would halves that were entire still shun
The pull of this strange star?

(On Amazing grace)

I WONDER WHAT WE'LL LOOK LIKE WHEN WE'RE OLD

The days that pass pass not through us alone,
But have their weight and measure, and these hours
That melted frowns and furrows also own
The pow'r to make new faces out of ours.
The virgin freshness of a child full-grown
Can in unending growing grow beyond
An op'ning bloom, and this small head so known
Can alter at the tapping of this wand.
Yet will the cherub smile, in which the rays
Of unmade light were one day made to pass,
Pass on into the usury of days
And in the woman shine not from the lass?
When hours have drawn again a line or two,
Will there be light within a later you?

15/2
(Hirael bay)

We live today tomorrow's yesterday,
And this one happy hour will sleep in peace
Within the little cells where moments stay
A long, long while, awaiting a release.
We hold within the markings of past hours
And feel them pass again, their warmth to share,
Yet they are there, for they are ever ours,
And as we let them be they will be e'er.
O sister, there are rays of joy that come
That make in us their dwelling; there are sighs
That will be heaved again, and there are some
Dim distant morrows in this evening's skies,
For we must grow, but growth is made of days,
And we are made of many yesterdays.

28/2
(Ash Wednesday, Penmon)

DEWI SANT

Dewi,
Pray for this our land,
Place on us your hand,
And be near.

Dewi,
Pray that we may see,
Pray that we may be,
Truly be.

Dewi,
Gwalia lân recalls;
Wales this night still calls
For your word.

Dewi,
Think of this our home,
Think on this your home,
Your own home .

Dewi,
Hear the voice of years,
Hear the ancient tears,
And return.

(Sung at Mass, chaplaincy, 1/3)
(On specially composed melody)

THE WIND, THE WIND!

And did you, Dewi, hear these seas?
Did you once listen to this breeze
And see one hour what this hour sees
        On this horizon?

Did you too, Dewi, know the pain
Of seeing glory one day wane,
Of wanting days to come again
        O'er this horizon?

And were you, Dewi, very near
This day, this hour, to days so clear
That as you stood they held no fear
        'Neath your horizon?

Did you upon this day draw nigh
To where it dawned? Did you too sigh
To see the morn that broke on high
        Fill your horizon?

And where you are beyond these seas,
Do you at times still hear the breeze
That brings the wind of many pleas
        To your horizon?

(On Qui es-tu, Roi d'humilité?)

I CARRIED IT IN THE TOP BREAST POCKET...
(St David's night, after the two Masses)

What will speak on when we can speak no more
Will speak through this dumb mouth, will whisper word
On quiet word, as each was formed before,
As oft as these dim lines may yet be heard.
But that this speech should come not from one breast,
That it should come from where another beat
One time, long, long ago; that it should rest
Upon this point that felt that gentle heat –
Thine own, sweet passing being, who'll pass not
Into the past without a voice to hold
Henceforth thy laugh from being for e'er forgot –
Is this perhaps a whispering too bold
To be reheard? Are there some words ne'er meant
On other list'ning hearts to be e'er spent?

More than Meaning

There is a meaning that no word can hold,
And messages that air can not maintain
Will pass through other pores, where truth untold,
But only known, is known at once again
Within another soul. There is a peace
Within the gentle feeling of a sound
That need not have a name, which need not cease,
But in some chasm of yearnings long redound.
A truth is held in many, many ways,
But much was lost in grasping, for the sense
Of touching absolutes is dimmed by rays
That fill the eye and ear with glare too dense.
For we are open when at last we close
Ourselves, and ne'er alert save in repose.

HAVING YOUR VOICE...

When parts of us can travel through the air
And leave the rest behind; when what we say
Can through these cogs and wheels yet linger there
While Sound's own organs wander far away;
When we can sing a song, and hear a sigh
Long hours beyond its ending; when we know
That our heart's tears another eye will cry
And that burnt days can on this band still glow,
Then we do well to think what trace we leave
On this our staggered present, we do well
To see the parting hours one hour can cleave
And think how heav'n ungrasped is deeper hell.
And yet when there will be no more to hold,
Will there be no use for a spark so old?

COLOPHON
(at Hebrew examination)

They tell me that the sages long ago
Made use of signs and squiggles such as these
To utter messages for all to know,
And now I know why so few heard their pleas.

AMONG THE HIPHILS

There are some gentle sounds
That trembling lips would stutter
That other limbs can utter
When no great noise abounds,
And in a quiet touch
Of being against being
Two minds can hear a meaning
Without their hearing much.

There are some little things
That are best said when silence
Can make heard its own eloquence
And voice moves not, but clings,
And there are parts of speech
That need obey no grammar,
That run in ways irregular,
That depth to depth can teach.

And when there is no sense
But only pulse of feeling
And moments of long healing
That carry long years hence,
There is a passing stream
Of knowing in soft holding,
Of hearing in beholding
The rays of Love's fair beam.

(On a French tune my brother used to sing,
to be found on one disc he made: *Y Ffoadur.*)

Hiphils: The hiphil, piel and poel are intensive forms of the Hebrew verb.

WE DON'T FEEL TIME WHEN WE'RE TOGETHER
(Benllech bay)

What is a drop of Time in this great sea
Of ebbing moments that come ne'er again?
What is the measure of Eternity
Where stars forget to turn and moons to wane?
What is the length of moments here below
Where little ticks can tap out such great things
And 'tween two beats ne'er one same rhythm show
As one heart groans and one heart softly sings?
Where are the moments that we left behind
When we 'gan to feel nought else pass but this
One wave on wave of knowing what can bind
Shared seconds in a passage of shared bliss?
And is Eternity so very long
When untraced hours ill hold but one brief song?

A PRESENT
(for Tina's mother)

A page can hold a mighty weight of thought
Still hovering unheard, untapped, unknown
Until a passing retina has caught
The current there contained, but not there shown.
And when a page with pages is combined
Until in dense array they thickly stand,
There lurks between two covers here entwined
A force that can control the holding hand.
A volume can sleep on and on and on,
As can the mind that thought it, or it can
Without a word redo the work once done
With no more voice or noise or effort than
It had to give when 'twas giv'n once a brain
That would ne'er think, but would hold all thought's strain.

9/3
(Library)

THE FUTURE DOESN'T EXIST

Tomorrow never trod upon this earth,
And Now was only Then at its own death,
Which never happened, for there is but birth
Of virgin seconds, each of which here saith,
"I pass thee on, for Passing is my name,
But I am in my brethren, who will hold
The Nowness of thy present much the same
As I have done with touching hands of old."
The æons that have been and that will be
Were all by moments held, and we hold all
In this hard squeezing of Eternity,
For though the time draws on and us doth call,
There is a little corner in this hour
In which to shelter from the moment's pow'r.

A QUESTION
(Eglwys Cwyfan)

When but a sound can change a life or two
And one unuttered word can utter all
That can or need be said, that sound may do
Its uttermost with flutterings so small –
When there is but a waiting for a breath
On which the wings of unfledged angels rest,
When in a pause are poised the life and death
Of all the little ones that could here nest –
Then there is in a silence something dense
That is not of the earth, there is a touch
Of something more than flesh when sense can sense
The feel of moving Soul in movements such
That though but little moves, the world revolves
Around a little sound that lives dissolves.

YOU'RE VERY SILENT
(Beneath the stars)

What 'tis to hold a little world enclosed
Within the arms that bear the weight of love,
What 'tis to know that two hearts have reposed
Their deepened years in one hour seen above
But never hoped or dreamt by two below;
What 'tis to feel the feeling of a soul
Breathed in an yielded breath, what 'tis to know
That in a tiny ball the world is whole –
This only virgin need that never shed
Its uttermost before can have the pow'r
To sense, for that but senses never wed
Or stroked, but only hurt, can know this hour.
There are more words in silence that is deep
Than in the fairest sounds no pain did weep.

An answer

When in the dark we walk without a light
Save one small lamp of faith; when one faint cry
Bears up the prayer of two into the Height
Of unseen Vision; when the ancient sky
Looks down with its old silence on the land
Where mortals live and love while laugh they may;
When on the edge of Wanting two souls stand
Awaiting but a word that would all say,
Then there are many years within the folds
Of one small envelope that one day sent,
And in the messages that dumb ink holds
The earth to Heav'n a voice hath somehow lent.
For though we were alone, we were well known,
And could not give what we did never own.

AND IT'S ALL TRUE

There was a maiden who once loved a lad
Who loved her too, and knew her loving well,
And these two lovers their own secret had,
For never could they of their loving tell.

Hid in the fields of Erin there are hearths
Where burns an ancient flame, lit long ago
By servants of the Lord who walked these paths
And taught this land the words its sons still know.

But in these homesteads there are also hid
At times some other ancient flames whose heat
The Gospel could not quench, for none could rid
The heart of all the pow'rs that in it meet.

And thus it was that families that prayed
And talked to Heav'n together could not talk
One to another, for some demon strayed
From long ago, and still was free to walk.

Such freedom was not giv'n to lad or lass,
Yet their hid loving found a way to roam:
At night two little lamps would let love pass
From yonder hilltop and from this strange home.

The moon did witness many happy hours
That parents never saw, and stars heard lays
That e'en the pain of Longing never sours
As day by day are lost our drifting days.

The maiden moved away, yet loved the lad
With fondest wanting that could never wane,
And in her lonely hours she was so sad
That she did tell her pen of all her pain.

The messages across the sea would pass,
And would on eagle's wings return, to warm
The little heart of this sweet little lass
Who little sensed the coming of the storm.

For soon the clouds would gather in the air
That no more brought her word, that no more knew
What had become of one small face so fair
That it alone her loving could e'er woo.

There was no sound across the Irish sea,
But only ripples of a fading past,
While here a newer wanting made a plea
For all her loving in a love to last.

And last it did, for never was it there.
It was in Erin still, where wiser years
Had judged it best to leave the missives where
They had arrived, lest they made known their tears.

For letters came and went between old hands
That held the leaves of love, and them consigned
To baskets that withheld two lonely lands
From meeting in a cross with kissing signed.

Without a heart the lad did also make
A match that would make children, but not love,
And knew not how this silence well to take,
And but presumed that some hand held his dove.

When time had moved along, two truths were known:
There had been words of love, but never ears
Or eyes to see their beauty, and alone
In lonely wedlock tears had filled the years.

And yet a spark of Erin's flame still burns
In one soul bid to be, in one small heart
Tapped into being by these many turns
Of hurried Fate that bad two dreams depart.

And it's all true! – "It's so beautiful! It's so beautiful! And it's all true!" (Tina's mother's words, between her tears – the which, apparently, are normally very rare. "And because my mother was crying, I was crying too.")

THEY'VE HAD THEIR TIME.
THIS IS OURS.
(Ynys Tysilio)

'Twas but a day, another, only one,
That made their last today a yesterday
That would hang in the air while this same sun
Returned and went, returned and went its way:
For on each silent stone there is a cry
That few e'en pause to heed; there is an hour
Engraved on every grave wherein a sigh
Let out a living's breath to æons dour.
And could we lift the lid off this long home,
Would we detect a ticking 'twixt its walls,
As 'twere of one great pendulum with some
Eternal tapping that with each tick calls,
For e'er, for e'er, is it for e'er?
For ne'er, for ne'er, for thee is it for ne'er?

ONE DAY IT WILL STOP BEATING
(Ynys Tysilio, 1st of May)

A beat, a beat, another beat of love,
Unheard, unnoticed, yet unwearied still
Propelling soul and body while above
The Will that bid it beat nods on until
It give one beat, one other, ere it rest
From tapping out life's time – one beat, I say,
One small beat at a time is His behest,
Yet this weak engine doth all hell delay,
For there is mighty pain where heav'n is near,
And what an hour can hold no years can fill.
So patter on, sweet heart, e'en though I hear
But one, but one, but one beat coming still . . .

Should one sound no more come, would anything
Again in this Creation ever sing?

A RAREFICATION OF HUMANS
(Ynys Cwyfan)

The world is made of many little worlds
That in their own small orbit turn and turn.
The books of History record not words
That change not this Earth's course, that none need learn,
But that are for one being volumes whole
Containing all the matter of his thought
And all that matters to one little soul
That in this vast Creation mattered nought.
There is within the womb of Time a home
Wherein one took his rest, there is a place
Where child could father meet, and no more roam
Unguided on this lonely planet's face.
There is a mother in the daughter's smile
That says but little, and but waits awhile.

UNUSED

The moments that contain the blessèd touch
Of unused joy, of newness now too fresh
To think of growing old or growing such
As age can make some grow, with o'ergrown flesh –
These moments will still hold what now we are
When they have changed our form, and all the years
That move with cosmic rays from star to star
Will not remove two heart-beats from our ears.
For there are some who tasted little joys
And played a game with something they knew not,
Who in their ageing childhood sought new toys
While what pleased not the eye was soon forgot.
When minutes have made furrows, will there be
No feeling in the pores that felt for me?

DEAR OLD P.J., THE SCENE OF MANY STRUGGLES!
(Eve of first examination)

There are too many pains upon this road
That 'tis our turn to tread; there are still sighs
That linger in the air that once bestowed
A breath of living 'neath these Cambrian skies
That pass along unruffled by the sound
Of hominids in pain. Again we hear
The silence of hard thought where thoughts unfound
Can not be traced in time as th'hour draws near. . .
The hour, the hour that our own mothers raced,
Unhurried dawdles past these last that run
The course that many many feet have traced
Upon this track of labours never done.
Why is the haste of ages never taught
To think awhile what meaneth all this thought?

Dear old...: My mother's words, after asking where the examination was.

A LADY DIED LAST NIGHT

A little child of God that made no noise,
And heard no sound across cemented ears,
For one short hour held two dimmed eyes in poise
Wide open with blind gaze. The tunnelled years
That passed thee wholly by had one small light
That no one else would see, for 'twas thine own,
And thy hid world of feeling had its sight
That ne'er was known, for ne'er could it be shown.
But in this hour, dumb sister, something stirred
Within thy sealèd soul, and something moved
Before thy seeing eyes. Some thing was heard,
For e'en we heard its echo: one night proved
The truth that had no voice: – thine only friend
Who came no more, came once more, at the end.

A lady: She was deaf and dumb, and blind by the end. She had one
close friend, her cousin. She sat up suddenly after he had died,
even though she had no means of knowing of the death. She made
as if to talk to someone and her eyes were gazing in one direction.
The only one who, though out of reach, mattered to her must
have come for her. She followed him that night.

The prophet

Will there be light again upon this land
That heard the rushing Wind come o'er its hills
Not once nor twice before, as th'ancient Hand
That folded mount and vale bade rocky wills
Be shattered oft 'neath this one gentle Touch
That comes from the unknown? Will there be praise
Borne on these deepened tones that can move such
As are not rocked by words? Are there yet days
That have been viewed beneath the eastern skies
Where Vision has its screens and Knowledge knows
What can but be, that will by western eyes
Be seen again? This little flame that glows
Upon this planet's shore has glowed before,
For 'tis the Egryn fire that others saw.

9/6
(after hearing what been given in words
of knowledge regarding Wales)

98

IN FLIGHT
(Salzburg)

What 'tis to know and never to have seen,
To feel without a touch, to hear no sound
And yet to be aware that one has been
With one hid distant presence closely bound,
Only the soul outpoured in gentle streams
Of living ink can prove, for there are hours
That strike not at one blow, yet carry dreams
In their stray wandering 'tween our thinking pow'rs.
O little soul unknown, yet deeply known,
What body holds thy sweetness, what fair eyes
Transmit that presence that but marks have shown
To one who now drawn by them walks the skies
That staggered long our thinking, held our thought,
And bade it drift 'twixt cloud and cloud thus caught?

Pain

O angel, shall not we behold the light
Of molten love that flowed from breast to breast?
Will the unknown yet now escape the sight
Of our awakened eyes, and shall here rest
The dreams of all our yesterdays unshared?
Do many morrows lie 'neath eastern seas
Of nought but wantings made? Are we ensnared
By what stray hours have found 'mid yearns like these?
O heart of Man, vast cosmos of a soul,
What pow'rs of pain lie 'tween thy pulsing walls!
These little valves that tap the ages' toll
Feel too each aching second as it falls
Upon the senses of the great abyss
Within this inward hell of wanted bliss.

4/7
(Rhyl)

LITTLE MOTHER

There are but holes within the human soul,
Made each of hollows deep. There are but yearns
That travel in the wake of minutes whole
In which we were complete. The infant learns
Upon his mother's breast where is his home,
And there are some who seek not love's full care
Till they have grown to trust. Yes, there are some
Who ne'er shall trust, for never was trust there.
O angel, I had trusted, I had felt
The feeling of a meeting never met
Within the wait of years, yet as we knelt
Together 'neath the Cross, some feeling yet
Was somehow left unfelt, for there was more
That we both knew, for we had loved before.

11/7
(St Benedict)

HALVED

But once and once alone are souls here wed,
And halves have but one other. There can be
No iterating of some words once said,
And access there is none to parts of me
Where one alone did tread. There is no face
That can light up again with fondling cheer
The chasmèd cold within; there is no grace
Of human kind that will find echo here.
For there is depth beneath the deepest need
That cannot be filled twice, nor twice be shown,
And there are stirrings that no ear may heed
Save hers who stirred them. For we stir alone
For one, one only being in this game,
And Love has not a meaning, but a name.

ALL THROUGH THE NIGHT

Ὄμματα εἰσίν ἀστέρες,
διά νυκτός,
δόξης ᾿όντες δή ᾿οπτήρες,
διά νυκτός,
ἡ σκοτία γάρ φως ᾿έστιν
ἐν τὸ καλόν ᾿ένεστιν·
τὸ ᾿αόρατον πάρεστιν
διά νυκτός.

Χάριν δε και ᾿έχει ᾿ούτος
διά νυκτός,
᾿Ω ᾿αστήρ καίπερ τοσούτος·
διά νυκτός,
᾿ισχυρός ᾿εί και ᾿αρχαίος,
και ᾿ημείς τούτου τού φωτός
᾿έσμεν ᾿αυγή ᾿εις ᾿αλλήλους
διά νυκτός.

(Melody: *Ar hyd y nos*)

Eglwys Cwyfan

Is this the place where two were once but one
And in a word withheld were many more?
Are these the stones where all was left undone,
Where all was known of Knowing's still locked store?
Is this the wood that held thy weight on mine,
Small child, that heard me hum thee to thy sleep
Of trust in him that rocked thee? Was it thine,
The voice that bid two dreamers patience keep?
O ecstasy of moments! Why are these
Strewn on the course of ages, to dull all
The calmer morrows that must needs must please
With norms of pain? Is it that they may call
Without a voice from stones that will remain
To speak of what once softened this long pain?

ABSENNOL

O wyry fwyn, a dd'wedaist ti Amen
I'r weddi fud a gronnai yn ein bron?
A ddaeth munudau hud ein doe i ben
Ers inni rodio glannau'r ynys hon?
A wyddit, angel, rym dy eiryn mân
A roddai'n llaw yn llaw y cryfaf Un?
A syniet allu gair a thyner gân
A godai mor ddi-hid o fab a'i fun?
O dawel un, a wyddost ôl dy lais,
Aroglau dy nesâd – a'th ymbellhad:
Pa fodd y clwyfwyd oes gan anferth glais
Y cyffwrdd na fydd iddo fyth ddyfnhad?
Cans yn y dyfnder mae rhyw fyd ynghudd
Na welodd cyn dy ddyfod olau dydd.

3/8
(Eglwys Cwyfan)

PELYDRAU

Nid oes ond nos yn hen ffurfafen ddu
Y bröydd pell, nid oes na gwefr na chân
I newid tôn dragywydd yn un su
A deithiodd yn ddigymar lwybrau glân
Y gwacter lanwau'r oll cyn bod un bod
Ond hen fodolaeth grai ymennydd maith
Y Bardd ei hun, a wyddai sut i ddod
I ben ei freuddwyd ef, cyn llunio'i waith.
Nid oes ond rhyw ddistawrwydd yn y nen
Sydd heddiw fel y ddoe heb glust at sain
Ac atsain y taranu fu ym mhen
Yr un Meddyliwr praff a holltai'r rhain
Yn syniad a chysyniad ddaliai rym
Egydion ei anelu mwyaf llym.

Nid oes ond goslef yn yr oesoedd maith
Sy'n dal i droi.
Nid oes dychweliad byth ar hyn o daith;
Nid oes ond ffoi
Ymhellach ac ymhellach o'r mwynhad
A oedd yn bod
Heb gyfwng i'w barhad.

Pelydryn ydoedd unig leufer nos
Y bröydd pell.
Un sain a fu, a gludai acen dlos
Rhyw air oedd well
Na hedd mudandod hir y Triawd fu
Yn oedi dro
Cyn torri'r hirfaith su.

Eonau oedd yn grwando ar y creu
Am hir, am hir,
A sêr oedd unig dystion hyn o weu
Y gwir o'r gwir.
Nid oedd ond Un a wyddai hynt a rhawd
Achosion mân
Yr un ddiysgog Ffawd.

Munudau ydoedd mesur mwyaf mawr
Y bys fu'n troi
Peirianwaith creu diatal awr ac awr
Fydd yn crynhoi
Hyd orig eithaf Amser ffeithiau oll
Cyfrolau Bod
Fel un eiliedyn coll.

A bu rhyw wenu ym mherfeddion certh
Yr hirnos a wrandawai ar yr hedd
Nas torrwyd, ac nas profwyd, ac yn nerth
Yr un llygedyn gwawl a ddaeth o wedd
Yr hen Ddihenydd, daeth ergydion mud
Ei grebwyll cryf i gyffwrdd â holl fro
Bodolaeth, ac yn nheimlad hyn o hud
Ysgogwyd tonfedd llewych yn ei thro.
Pelydryn ydoedd egni'r pethau mân
A deithiai cledrau bychain trefn y rhod,
Ac yn y ddawns fu'n dechrau gyda chân
Y Cerddor mud, death corau'r nen i fod.
Ond nid oedd digon yn nigonedd llwyr
Breuddwydiwr engyl yn eonau'r hwyr.

Bu cyffro yn nistawrwydd gwacter hen
Y dyfnder maith,
Ac ym mhelydrau tawel mwynaf wên
Y Meistr gwaith
Death ton at don o egni brau i roi
Gronynnau'r byd
Ar daith eu hen hen droi.

Ond gweld ymhell wnaeth golwg Awdur sêr,
A thros y ffin
A rannai bröydd tranc a bröydd pêr
Nef hawdd ei thrin,
Canfuwyd rhawd pelydrau coll y rhod
Na ddeuent byth
At ben eu taith a'u nod.

Bu oedi yn yr oesau cyn eu dydd,
Ac oedi hir,
Ac yn effeithiau eithaf ffeithiau cudd
Penodau'r gwir,
Caed hunllef yn y llef a roddai fod
I'r geiryn mud
A wnâi i'r oesoedd ddod.

Nid oes modd gwybod pa beth wybu'r Un
A wybu'r oll,
Ac nid oes olwg ar gyflawnder llun
Lle nad â 'ngholl
Manylyn un manylyn sydd â'i ran
Yng nghyfres gref
Y mân achosion gwan.

Ond gwelwyd Heddiw cyn bod sôn am Ddoe,
Ac yn y treiddio llym a'r syllu hir
I rawd na wyddai egwyl fer na hoe,
Fe gofiwyd cyn ei fod ddiffeithwch tir
A yswyd wedi llif yr oesoedd brau
Gan ynni'r un pelydryn dasgai dro
Ar lwyfan yr amserau deithiai'n glau
O fro'r tawelwch i ryw newydd fro.
A bu Yfory yn cymylu'r wawr
Cyn geni'r munud cyntaf: bore byd
A ofnai ychwanegu awr at awr
Na fyddai'n oedi byth, na'n troi mewn pryd.
Bu gwybod gormod cyn bod gwybod dim,
A bu ar roliau Amser ddarllen chwim.

Y mae i allu creu alluoedd mwy
A edwyn Ef,
Ac ym mhelydrau'i wên fe deimlái glwy',
A chlywai lef
Yn dod o bell, o bellter eithaf gwae,
Yn gweiddi, "Na!
Fel hyn, fel hyn y mae.

"Os crëir nef, fe grëir uffern dân,
Ac ni bydd mwy
Leihad na thranc ar rym pelydrau mân
Ddaw heddiw drwy
Y gofod oedd y ddoe yn fan ddi-boen
I Ti dy hun
Yn dy dragwyddol hoen.

"Ai gwell yw bod heb wybod, bod heb fod
Am byth, am byth?
Ai da yw rhoddi'r gallu, rhoddi'r nod,
Ynteu yn syth
Ymworthod â'r cydrannu, troi yn ôl
O'r tegan hwn
O syniad anferth ffôl?

"Oni bydd dim, ni fydd na lleddf na llon
Yng nghân y dydd,
Ac o ddyfnderoedd cudd y freuddwyd hon
Nid oes a fydd
Yn ateb i'r ymateb allai ddod
O hyn o nos
A fydd am byth yn bod."

A bu, a bu am byth, oleuni gwawr
Yn troi nos faith y gwagle'n llawnder cain
Lle'r erys atsain, lle'r aroglir sawr
O'r hyn a fu pan roddid sain at sain
I greu peiriannau trefn o ddeunydd crai
Y gwirioneddau mud. Bu gosod ton
A thonfedd ar belydrau grym di-drai,
A lleufer fu'n dadebru'r blaned hon.
Bu gweld yn y gweladwy, yn yr un
A deimlodd wres y bore, ac a fu
Yn dod i oed, yn gwybod gwawdd ei fun,
Fu'n llon yn hen symlrwydd pethau cu.
Ond mab i fab ei feibion ydyw hwn
Sy'n dwyn ar ei ysgwyddau ryfedd bwn.

Ni fydd na chwsg na gorffwys i fab dyn
Dan olau'r sêr,
Ac er hir dyfu nid yw'n tyfu'n hŷn
Nag engyl Nêr
A welodd holl ddynionach oesoedd byd
Yn chwarae'u rhan
Ar lwyfan ddeil o hyd.

Tegannau'r plentyn yw tegannau'r tad,
Ac un yw llid
Yr hogyn egwan a'r rymusaf gwlad
Sy'n troi'n ddi-hid
Fyddinoedd bychain pren y gemau mawr:
Un ydyw gwefr
Y bodlon yn ei awr.

Ym mhwysau bys y gorwedd pwysau byd:
Ysgytwad oes
Yw'r symud sydd yn symud oll ynghyd
Heb deimlo'r loes
Na'r clais ar ochrau'r cread sy'n parhau
Yn hynaf drefn
Y rhod fu'n llawenhau.

Nid oes na nerth nac angel yn y nef
A ŵyr paham
Y mynnai un fyddaru'r nen â llef
Yr olaf cam.
Nid oes wybodaeth am elfennau crai
Y crebwyll gwan
Ac eiliad cynta'i fai.

Y mae eiliadau na all oriau'r rhod
Eu dychwel at yr ennyd cyn eu tro
I ddianc o'r distawrwydd a roes fod
I dreigl dydd, ac ni all hedd y gro
Dawelu'r awel fain a rwygodd gnawd
Chwaraewr gemau drud ag egni rhad
Yr un pelydryn bychan a droes Ffawd
Ar hirfaith rawd achosion ei pharhad.
Ac nid oes dim goleuni yn yr hwyr,
Ond ôl yr hyn a fu ryw ddydd, ryw awr
Pan fu amserau'n bod, ond 'does a wyr
Pa bryd fu hyn, cans diffodd wnaeth y wawr.
A bu breuddwydio hir yn nyfnder hun
Y Triawd hen, ai hardd fai hyn o lun.

Awst, 1990

ABBOT DYFRIG

Farewell, good father of a little world
That will turn through the ages yet to fall
Upon this hallowed acre where thy word
Bid rock from rock be hewn, and where thy call
Bid sons of unwed progeny be formed
To people this small desert, where some peace
Not made of sound still rests 'mid sounds deformed
By wearied song that knows not where to cease.
O home of many homeless, fatherland
Of children not the same, yet much the same,
Wilt thou no longer see this little hand
That with one finger called without a name
And ruled a silent troop as it moved on
And on and on t'ward where one more has gone?

TAIZÉ

(6 km from Cluny)

Upon this little ball that spins us all
There are some dots that were not seen to move
But were beheld for long ere e'er things small
Began to grow and grow, as 'twere to prove
The pow'r of watered growth. There are designs
Well marked and studied by the eye of man
That were observed to falter, while here shines
The ray of Blessing that no brain did plan.
There are some gusts of laughter blown this way
From long ago, from long before we were
Placed on this map, and 'tis an ancient play
That makes the spell of Beauty oft recur,
That its amusement hath where now we are,
And these refrains have travelled from afar.

THE EIGHTH

Could I have known what would not happen there
And seen the unforeseen before its head
Was for e'ermore unveiled and made to glare
Upon the track of years, could I have read
A chapter of this History before,
Would I upon a preface have spent all
And passed upon this day beyond that door
That led to the unknown? O! massive wall,
That parted youth and ageing, thou didst hide
The fact that thou wouldst crumble in an hour –
A little hour that bade the hours outside
In all their noise roll on 'neath their own pow'r.
Did we know of tomorrow on this day,
Would we take trouble to pass by this way?

TINA

What in a sound can lie, what in a name,
But he who loved can know, for he loved all
That in a call once to his vision came,
And learnt the mantra of a prayer so small
That none knew of its chatter save the one
Who called it forth, for both were incense sweet
That their own real presence did bid run
In wave on wave of wanting that all meet.
O meeting of all meanings in a word!
Could I have known the resonance of sound,
Would I upon a day have calmly heard
Two notes that now a symphony have found
That will play on until the beating heart
Can cope no more with harmonies that part?

'Sbwriel?

Pwy wybu hyn, pwy syniai am y byd
A fu fan hyn yn troi ar echel gudd
Ymhell o droeon oes, cans troi yn fud
Wnaeth dy fydysawd di, ac ar dy rudd
Nid oedd na rhych nac arwydd o'r mwynhad
Yr wylit am ei gael; ni chlywyd su
O'r unig lef fu'n llefain am foddhad
Yn nyfnder dwfn y fron a'r aeddfed fru.
O angel cudd, a grwydraist hyn o rawd
Heb ddangos deigryn mân yr oriau maith,
A ddaeth dy gri drwy ddiofalwch Ffawd
Heb reswm yn y byd i ben ei daith
Dan fron a glywodd hir hir lef dy fron,
Ac a ddaw un i grwydro'r Eden hon?

28/10
(wrth ddarllen barddoniaeth Elisabeth fach)

I COULDN'T BELIEVE IT
("When I woke up this morning I couldn't feel any pain at all.")

We did but use our head and lips and heart
In this unstudied surgery; – though two hands
Were in two others held, 'twas not the art
Learnt by Hippocrates that loosed the bands
Of ancient pain. We knew not how to word
The formula that worked the magic spell
Of which from friend and friend we had just heard,
Yet 'twas enough to know that Heav'n knew well.
We knew that we were heard, yet we knew not
That Might was thus at hand, nay that hands held
The Hand that held the Dynamis forgot
By cultured faith, that daring prayer withheld.
We were surprised, for we dared not to hope,
And did but fumblingly with this Thing grope.

I couldn't believe it...: Student's words the following day.

(Karen's healing took place after we had prayed before the
Blessed Sacrament, through the intercession of St Winefride
and St John Roberts.)

L. B.

(Dom Laurence Bévenot, my spiritual father)

There is a little lamp that will not burn
Again upon our shore, there is a source
From which no more can flow, nor shall return
Another page charged with semantic force
Across the skies that ne'er could hold apart
A father from his child. There is a hole
Within this universe where one small heart
Has missed a beat and lost hold of a soul.
There are but decomposings in the land
That holds the gentle head that made of Song
The paradise of ears, yet one kind hand
Did in its fingers grip what lingers long.
For though, my father, time now beats thee too,
There will be echoes of what thoughts could do.

2/11
(All Souls)

I WANT TO BE BURIED HERE
(16th November, Penmon)

When we are gone, when we are gone,
What sound will linger gently on,
What will be found when work is done,
      And we are gone?

When days have passed, when days have passed,
What hours of these our hours will last,
When we ourselves have anchor cast,
      And days have passed?

When waves still roll, when waves still roll,
What unborn lover will here stroll,
When ancient song floods one more soul,
      And waves still roll?

When bells still chime, when bells still chime,
What little feet will our bliss climb,
When we have yielded stolen time,
      And bells still chime?

When we sleep on, when we sleep on,
Will there be singing where grace shone
On myriads whose lone chant is done,
   And who sleep on?

When nothing more, when nothing more
Of this our ripple laps the shore
Of Penmon, will what went before
   Do nothing more?

     (On specially composed melody)

A FRIEND, A FRIEND

When there is one to whom the heart is known,
Who senses every ripple, every wave
Of thought hid in the mind that thinks alone
Within this lonely world that no thought gave
For many pains unheard; when there is one
Who feels the tear unshed, who reads the word
Emitted by the brain when e'en the sun
Did look away and nothing saw or heard,
Then there is an oasis in the stars,
A place where something matters, there is here
A corner of Eternity where scars
Have time to heal, and where there can draw near
Two worlds within a universe too vast
To notice little seconds ticking past.

GWAHODDIAD
(gan yr Esgob)

A welir eto olau ar y bryn?
A welir haul Yfory lle bu Doe
Yn goffadwriaeth faith o'r pethau hyn
A fu un tro, cyn i ddiwrnodau ffoi
Ar ryfedd daith, heb bwrpas a heb nod
Ar wyrdroadau Ffawd, dan ddellni hen
Holl ddigwyddiadau diymarbed Bod
Na throesant fyth yn ôl? Oes yma wên,
O hen Ddihenydd? Ai hwn ydyw gwawl
Dy syllu hir ar lwybr troellog byr
Crwydradau'n dydd? Ai tybed at dy fawl
Y'n tynnwyd ni yn ôl i'r lan lle tyr
Pelydryn dros y gorwel lle bu rhai
Yn canu hen ganeuon am a wnâi?

5/12

Un ange inconnu
(Immaculate Conception)

There is a little angel that the world
Knows nothing of, that fluttered from beyond
Imagination's hope, and swiftly whirled
Away to whence it came. Some magic wand
Did tap the fairest soul that could have been
And bid it be, and gave it form to hold
The wonder of a being never seen
Within this lonely vale of tears untold.
It will be said that this is blasphemy,
That one in Sion was the fairest maid,
And yet there was but one that was for me
From Beauty moulded and for my soul made.
And I perceive that I am bound to be
A part of what I was ere I felt thee.

רֹאשִׁי רֹאשִׁי
(End of term present)

There is in death's dark vale where many wait
The big big dagesh that will end it all
A small oasis where the mighty weight
Of Hithpaels can be allowed to fall
Upon the shoulders of a kindly friend,
A fond Gamaliel at whose size ten feet
A horde of yeladim regrets the end
Of two short hours of berachoth too sweet.
There is a head that carries many things
And knows whereof they're made. The very roots
That 'neath thick mystery lie he to light brings,
And this Zelotes with much cake recruits
The generations that go on holam
And leholam with scarce a yod of harm.

רֹאשִׁי רֹאשִׁי: My head, my head

LOVE SANDWICH

In many forms can meaning move
From breast to breast, and matter holds
The trav'lling thought that pulsing love
Without a word enfolds, unfolds.

In many ways can two rays meet,
Can feelings without touch be felt.
There is a warmth in one heart's heat
That does each day another melt.

In many nothings things are said
And unseen acts are studied long.
The mother and the bride unwed
Sing well the hidden carer's song.

The meaningless means more to me
Than words too loud to be heard well,
And in a taste I can taste thee,
And on thy well-stored love I dwell.

(On specially composed melody)

WAITING IN THE LIBRARY

The world is full of eyes, and eyes are full
Of looks of different meanings. Each new smile
And frown a tale of weal and woe doth pull
In its deep wake, and every gaze awhile
Withholds what we behold to be within
Where no one walks save one, who is alone
With many decibels of unheard din
That never had a voice except its own.
The world is full of feet that walk and walk,
Yet one sole patter ends the roving yearn
That hears not sound in song nor truth in talk
For that it did in gazing this once learn,
That of all faces one alone would shine,
That but one could e'er utter, *You are mine*.

HELP

And when the tears of many waiting years
Would gush through little borings in the soul
Tight-sealed again by safe, sure-locking fears
That now the great automaton control,
There is in one unuttered sentence all
That need be said, and in the shortest word,
The tetragram of pain, resounds one call
Wherein the deepest depth of Man is heard.
O little, little thing, O human heart,
Wast thou made big enough to hold the strain
Of cosmic Hurt, and was there ever art
To lessen for an hour the oldest pain?
O Craftsman of the years, Thy sentinels
Were sent in time to hold some blast that swells.

DIARY

A little book of History unwrit
Rests in the hand that day by day will fill
Its virgin sheets with facts, as bit by bit
The possibles of Truth that hover still
Within Tomorrow's air are made to be
Irrevocably cast. Indelible
The ink that will trace what one Eye can see
E'en now in this strange script invisible.
O harmless thing, that silently dost lie,
Dost thou hold marks of torture, throbs of bliss,
Or pages of long waiting, where no eye
Will think to look again, for 'twas of this,
The ordinariness of passing time,
That tome and tome was writ, with scarce a rhyme?

Y MAE YN FY NGALLU...
(It is in my power...: Bishop's words)

What can lie in a word so very small
Is of a weight so huge that other sounds
Are drowned e'en by the silence that doth call
For its slow coming, for within the bounds
Of one short syllable there lies a life,
Perhaps two lives, perhaps the lives of lives
Whose echoes faint may last when once the strife
Of knowing not has known what Heav'n contrives.
There are some little sounds, some little signs
Marked on the silent page that blast the world
In which our dreams revolve. The pen entwines
The strokes of unheard meaning where is hurled
The venom and the kiss of utterness
That travels through the air to curse or bless.

ANTINIA
(For a St Dwynwen's card)

Within the soul there is another soul
That should have been, that could have been therein,
And that is there by absence, for the whole
Of Man was felt when it was found within
Th'encounter of unseens: th'unseen of two
That saw the shapeless soul shaped perfectly
For it alone, th'unseen that saw the true
Beholding of a being where were three.
We are a little lonely on this globe
Where many noises fade when but one voice
Can mean that meaning that alone can probe
The emptiness within. And yet the choice
To hold not on to this that has no hand,
But only touch, must for one lifetime stand.

3/1/91

You'll Always Have Me

To know that there is one who will be there
At hand, though far, far off; that there is one
Untouched, in touch with every hidden care
That can be heard by mother in the son
That she has nursed awhile; that there are eyes
That can look at a face and read the tome
Writ large, it seems, thereon; that unvoiced sighs
Can cross the seas and find their own way home:
This is to know that we shall not float on
Alone on Chronos' surf, unanchored here
By any cord of care; that when 'tis done
We shall not pass unhindered to the bier
That takes all time away, but shall again
Look into two blest eyes that stroked much pain.

ONE CAN DIE OF A BROKEN HEART

Could other hands e'er touch the sacred pores
That felt the softest pulse of beating love?
Could other fingers know again what stores
Each well-known spot and furrow where now move
Th'antennæ of the soul, the little limbs
That without sound sound deepest depth within
By touch of ink or blood? For here nought skims
Unthinking o'er the feeling felt therein.
There was a lady nursed by thee, whose son
Came, came again as older she did grow,
As he had ever come, and when the sun
That in her shone was dimmed, life lost its glow.
And as he could not live and did not live,
Nor could I see thee this to others give.

7/1
(Llanddwyn and Llangwyfan)

ONE DAY YOU'LL DO AS DID RONSARD'S FRIEND

When gold to silver has with ageing turned
And these same eyes look out upon a world
That has grown older too; when days have burned
The fuel of their first yearning, wherein whirled
Ecstatic minds in love, will these two lips
Their impish smile still make; will this same face
Through wearied skin still shine as slowly slips
The radiance of thy morn apace, apace?
Can angels age with æons; can there be
Less warmth within the heart made all of care?
And when the years have cut their lines in thee,
These features that mean all, will they be there?
And will that cherub-look look back awhile
At old fond words, and, looking, give a smile?

Ronsard: He wrote that one day she would say, "Ronsard me chantait au temps où j'étais belle..."

THE DISINTEGRATION OF FARNBOROUGH

See how these Christians love each other well,
And better still when all the wicked world
Has been cast out of this most blessed hell
That cloisterers enclose in one vast word.
Contemplative hoodwinks some multitude
Of prayerful sins, and contemplation holds
The leisure to perceive in solitude
The fissures that proximity unfolds.
We are too well to be too well beheld,
And gazing at each other we see all
That art theatric has for years withheld
From lesser mortals who ne'er had a call
To rise, rise up, rise high, rise higher still
To apatheia's heights, where some fall ill.

Farnborough: "There must be something brewing and positively sizzling. "Write an amusing poem about it and send it to me." (Dom Alban, writing from Prinknash, 7th January, 1991.)

DAETH BACHGEN YN ÔL I'R YSGOL I DDWEUD "FFARWÈL"

Wilt thou return, young soul; wilt thou return
From this far land, and from lands farther still
Whence none can come again? What wilt thou learn
In this thy further schooling? 'Tis but will
That, given to another, bids thee walk
Where thy heart would not go, for its own beat
Could have gone on awhile as gentler talk
Directed t'wards the aisle thy wayward feet.
The bell that counts this midnight counts the blood
That in young veins still flows, still flows, still flows
A little closer to the stagnant flood
Of piercèd Pain, that its blest dream bestows.
For many wait upon that lotus shore
Who hurried their eternity before.

15/16/1
(War declared at midnight)

Daeth...: "A boy came back to school to say 'Goodbye'."

DIVORCE

'Tis strange, 'tis oddly strange that love can be
So different from itself, so unlike all
It was to be, and yet could it this see,
Could it behold the moments that appal
Our wiser days, would it e'en yet withhold
The right to be – the right to be awhile,
A little while that would a risk enfold
Within the rapture of a first spring smile?
Was it in vain that love was let to flow
Into the blossoming of little
lives That will e'en in the winter grow and grow
Until they know the bliss whence pain derives?
We are a little hasty with a kiss,
For there are many hours ahead of this.

Divorce: Written after hearing of the tragedy at the minister's house.

LOYALTY

The world is full of tears, uncaught, unknown,
Unseen e'en by the ones that bid them be,
Who entered not the regions where alone
We are all that we are. For History
Is made of unwrit chapters, where some read
Uncounted episodes where angel eyes
Alone were let to peep, to weep the deed
That in great dumbness cried unto the skies.
The pity of it, that the hearts that know
What 'tis to be well loved, what 'tis to love
Can on the hardest rock their warmth bestow
And with the deepest pow'rs can nothing move . . .
It is not fair, this game, this wildest game
That calls all Hell and Heav'n by one same name.

IT'S LIKE A TEMPLE

There are some folds of earth that hold a heav'n
Enclosed in inches square; there are some parts,
Some corners of the Cosmos where were giv'n
Stray particles of bliss, and there are hearts
That pant again where others patter by
Detecting nothing of a something hid
By one or two beneath some sleeping sky
That woke not to disturb what Folly did.
There are some molecules where linger still
Soft emanations, radiations such
That e'en the shields of deep metallic Will
Take in, for these move in with scarce a touch.
Is this perhaps why spirits rove again
Upon the shore' tween weal and waiting pain?

Temple: reference to car.

Spirits rove...: According to the Purgatory Manuscript, some departed souls do part of their Purgatory on the spot where they have incurred it.

HE DEPARTED WITHOUT BEING DESIRED

To know that we know not what shall befall
Our unmarked tracks, to lie in limbo long
Without a word, with nothing heard at all,
Is to love much yet to none to belong,
To want what may not be and yet may be,
To cling hard to a hope not fully snapped
And be for one more day at liberty
To be by someone, Someone, sometime trapped.
To be but wanted is to have a soul
That sparkled in the æons ju'st an hour –
The hour that was its own – for moments stroll
In aimless amble on when none would pour
A soothing sound upon th'unneeded one
That grew and wilted 'neath a hurried sun.

He departed...: 2 Chron 21, 20.

O LILI WEN FACH, O BLE DAETHOST TI?
(St Valentine)

I cannot be without a part of me
That is by hurting there when far away.
The hours that could have been no more may be,
For what was left unstirred could p'haps obey
The frozen will, the chill of chosen peace
From all that need intrude – but this strange thing,
The knowing that a being may not cease
To be half of the world, to Time shall cling.
O angel, had thy wings not spread their spell
Upon these little cells that chanced to hide
Beneath thine unsought flight, 'twould have been well,
Th'untroubled walk of strangers side by side.
But I have known thee, I have shown thee all,
And my unknowing may no more recall.

O lili wen fach...: "O snowdrop (Welsh, little white lilly), where did
you come from?"

RHODRI

Ni ddaw dros donnau'r awyr eto sain
Y cyfaill cudd, ni fydd tynerwch un
Yn ei gynhesrwydd brau yn treiddio'r rhain
Na'n cyrraedd mwy ei braidd di-lais, di-lun.
Bu rhyw newyddion drwg yn teithio'r tir
Y bore hwn sy'n ffin i ddeufyd maith
Y pethau sydd a'r pethau fydd yn wir
Yn unig yn eu hawr, er un yw'n taith.
A weli di, a deimli donfedd ddofn
Rhyw orsaf bell, fy ffrind, y noson hon,
Y gyntaf ddaw i'th ran ym mröydd ofn
Yr oesau, fu'n hir deithio'r estron don?
Ac wrth it fwrw golwg ar yr oll,
A deimli ddeigryn am dy Gymru goll?

16/2/91

144

MAM
(For Tina's mother)

Within a sound are found the bounds of home,
And 'neath a syllable the world is rocked
In old security as new tears come
To every little mother's womb unlocked
And made to hold its own, its very own,
At its own hour – the hour of many hours
That waited long, or yet long to be known,
For there are some not born to know birth's pow'rs.
What is the bond of ages? Is it this
'Tween mother and grown child, or is the gaze
That in the daughter sees the home of bliss
The ancient light that makes days cling to days?
What is the world when there is not a smile,
Or one to say, *I'll hold you for a while?*

THERE

When Thou art there, sweet Lord, there is no sound,
But only Presence felt, and every word
That from the Godhead comes, to flesh is bound,
In that in the event the Truth is heard
And every act bespeaks the fact to be
Reread for ever on the charts of years
That mark the turns that steered Eternity,
For 'tis in looking well that the heart hears.
When thou art there, sweet maid, at times there are
In sounds that fill the air some meanings sent,
But there are presences that can be far
From frightened breasts that know not what is meant.
For there are meanings that no sound can hold,
And there are stories that but One was told.

Mary and Martha, alas, have parted

What is the essence of the Great Divide
'Tween life within and life abundantly
In overflowing spilt? Who e'er did hide
The depth that was not there when constantly
The inward was without? And who saw not
The vast terrain within when but a word,
A look, a gesture, did unveil the spot
Where echoes of some Harmony were heard?
There are who flee their centre and are where
They need not always be, and yet there are
That o'er their utter being nothing wear
And yet that can draw gazes from afar.
For there is correspondence in the heart
That taps, Am I what others think thou art?

(The above was written after reading these words from Prink-
nash: "The thought of Farnborough leaves me sad. I spent some
of the happiest years of my long monastic life there, and I loved
their celebration of the liturgy (especially at Christmas and Holy
Week), and the choir on Sundays always gave me a spiritual lift.
Now, alas, Fr David and 4 others have gone to Oulton Abbey to
start a new life, leaving Fr Magnus and the rest to carry on. I can't
compete with your heavenly Muse, but here is something for a
comic strip. Can you add a second verse?

LAMENT FOR FARNBOROUGH

Mary and Martha, alas, have parted;
The row should really never have started.
Now Magnus reigns beneath the dome:
Will Mozart go? Guitars come home?
Fabian is now in Rome, mission uncompleted;
Farnboro' is left alone, sadly depleted.

Jeremiah.

Yours frivolous as ever, fr Alban.")

PEN

What can be touched by contact 'tween two things,
So quiet both, so dead when left to lie
Inanimate with neither breath nor wings
Upon this little desk, none but the eye
That listens to the sound of lines may know,
Nor may the sound perhaps be fully heard
Unless these shapes of meaning may bestow
Upon a hungry ear their choicest word.
I cannot touch what lies beyond the skies
But by this tool once touched by that same breast
That bid it henceforth rise and fall with sighs
Not of its own sweet making. Present blest
With presence of the absence of a soul,
Will one hour's touch from thee this pain control?

When there is but the sound of pain within
And in the air nought but the stillness full
Of knowing that sweet moments did begin
Once to be known; when starlit seconds pull
Not forward but back, back to where they paused
A little while, a very little while
That held the æons down, as 'twere uncaused
By cosmic Time, but by one cherub smile;
Then there is but one language that can hold
The heavy weight of void, there is but one
Last ancient grammar that may yet enfold
The meaning of a sigh, and, when 'tis done,
The pause that hid us may perhaps be found
Still lingering hard by some broken sound.

GOD HAS A PRESENT FOR YOU

There is an eye that saw the whole of Time,
And several times, ere it a measure had.
There is a pupil that watched æons climb
From chasmèd void to bliss where one thought bad
The story be: there is a brain that knew
The lengthy moment and the rapid age
Ere e'er the well-read future, coming new
To hominids' pale gaze, could mark this page.
And there is something, sister, in this earth
That bent the blind trajectories of hours
And in a plaintive song placed notes of mirth
To be perceived but once by carnal pow'rs.
And yet a grain of bliss can be twice bliss
When ere it pass a warning comes of this.

(On specially composed melody)

God has a present...: a word of knowledge.

CHILDREN

The Angles and the Saxons handed on
The sound of little things, the ancient name
That patted tiny heads in ages gone
The way of every age, and 'tis the same
Antiquity of sound that calls anew
The unborn morrow and the newest morn,
Fruit of a growing dream, that long nights knew
To be the fairest gift of youth's full dawn.
There is in trusting arms and weeping eyes
A depth that calls on depth; there is within
An angel clasp a force that rocks the skies
Of long and Stoic thought, that called truth sin.
For when a little world draws near us thus
We come too close to what is part of us.

3/5

(eve of Eva's marriage)

THE ONE WITH THE TIE

The light of Ars can burn across the years
And without stole or surplice shrive the heart
That basks in these old rays, for as it nears
The ancient shining many fears depart,
And limbs and sounds set free can tell a tale
That saints and hermits told with but the mind,
For well the walls of prayer hid from this Gale
The practised soul full formed to grind and grind.
That there should be a knowledge e'en now known
In this our time, in this our little land,
In this small space, for this name, this my own,
And that a saint of God should bid me stand
Beneath the waiting Pow'r, and let it fall,
This is to know the sadness of it all.

11/5
(after being called out specially
in a charismatic meeting)

Amid a rocking world there lingers yet
A sound or two unhurried to be moved
By rhythmic change, and ancient acts beget
New virgin lungs that learn not words improved
By bleeped computed wisdom, but things aged
With many ageings that recalled first days
From sleeping depths, as old scenes were restaged
On knees that once had crawled to these same lays.
There is a womb unopened, and there are
Some sounds unheard, some songs perhaps not meant
To be passed on o'er one line that afar
Did stretch – could stretch – these pulsings that are sent
From dawns that long have set, and yet still shine
Within a face that holds a power divine.

St John Roberts

(Eve of Pentecost)

O fab ein tir a thad ein tadau ni,
A gofi heno'r fan a'th gofia di?
A glywi gri mudandod maith yr oes
A wrendy osteg y canrifoedd roes
Eu maen am faen y beddrod lle bu hoen
A gras lle gynt y deliaist Waed yr Oen?
A glywi heno'n nafnau'r Aberth hen
Ryw newydd wanwyn,
 ryw gyfarwydd wên?

Child of our land, chaste father of a throng,
Dost thou this night recall to whom belong
These parts of earth that once to heav'n were wed,
These silent quires where once thy feet did tread?
Dost thou still hear the echo of this pause
In ancient song that long flowed 'tween the pores
Of heavy stone where buried lies awhile
A patient spring, an old familiar smile?

(On *Finlandia*, doubling final bars.
Written for Welsh Mass, Gellilydan.)

TIME STOPS FOR NO MAN.
OUR TRAUMAS COME AND OUR TRAUMAS GO.
(First final)

Almighty moments that fix all our marks
And carry off our chances without thought
For afterthoughts, for little hurting sparks
Of unignited points, O! seconds caught:
A second after you no longer were
Yet valid for your use, O! horrid boon
That flows and bears our blunders off for e'er
And bids the evening sigh that it were noon!
O! thing without a form that forms our all,
We know thee not except when we thee curse;
Thy little voice, thy little noise so small
But taps and taps and gently taps, No worse
Is this my present tap than tappings yet
Unwound in this great clock for ever set.

Time stops...: Tina's words before the examination.

156

Early Church History

Beyond the sky there burn so many stars
That twinkled here awhile, and warmed the earth.
Beyond the sky there burns yet what still mars
Æonic bliss, for long lives some short mirth
In what it could from Nemesis not steal.
Beyond the sky there are some scars well nursed,
Some dates recalled on which things 'gan to reel,
Some distant throbs of Time that all Time cursed.
Beyond, beyond, on yonder hid domains
There are some old, old hours that matter still
To some, and there somewhere perhaps are pains
Unthought that every thought can e'ermore fill.
And is there one sole mark for this one test
That none sat twice that was e'er damned or blest?

THE PICTURE

O little thing with wings that none can see
Save one that felt them pass, wilt thou still gaze
In framèd stillness from this spot that we
Trod once and tread again in these last days
That dawn o'er these same waves that echo yet
The meeting of two strangers on this shore?
Wilt thou smile on when years and years forget
The minutes that once tingled here before?
And when the great Unknown at length is known
And one of us no longer treads this land,
Will these big eyes that once read each thought shown
On annotated visage still here stand
And look and look into this looking-screen
That gazes at a gaze that once had been?

11/6
(Before final final and walk to first walk)

THREE MARKS SHORT
(of a first)

No longer are there means by which to gain,
Or moments left in which to win and win
The little ticks that could reduce the pain
Of knowing evermore that 'twas within
The grasp of passing hours to pass the line
Of excellence. And there are secrets known
Of knowledge undelivered that still pine
To have a hearing on a page unshown.
Eternity is judged on little hours,
And if the ache of nearness can be thus,
What gnaws the naked soul's untempered pow'rs
When one last breath breathes out the whole of us?
And does each passing second pass or fail
Some dying soul that 'gins to chant or wail?

St Wolfgang

A year and twenty more have here rung been
Since last this sight and scent and sound were known.
The telling of the hour when hours were green
Was not as this soft tolling of hours shown
Upon the score of Time. The wheels that turn
The cycles that begin to rebegin
Seem here to grate awhile, and bid me learn
That much beginning few great ends can win.
O little sound, wherein is bound the all
Of what is made or marred, will this thy chime
Tomorrow and tomorrow still recall
Dim moments of lost hours that travelled Time
Ere fears that thou couldst cease e'er crossed the mind
Of just another speck of human kind?

6/7
(under the belfry)

SAINT WINEFRIDE

Forwynig fythol fwyn, fe fuost gynt
Yn dân dros Grist ei Hun,
A gwenfflam oedd dy rawd a'th ryfedd hynt
Wrth ganlyn Mab y Dyn.
Ti fuost ffyddlon yng ngharwriaeth lem
Y galon na fynn roi
I fwy nag un, na bwrw eto'i threm
Ar eilun a fai'n troi
Ei grym oddi ar y Gwrthrych mwyaf un.

O gentle maid, white virgin of a day
That marked all days to come,
Thou too didst know the treading of a way
Found hard at times by some.
Thou too didst know, know well, what 'tis to burn,
But couldst not be aglow
By halves, by quarters – that could this flame turn
On more than one – nor show
What 'twas to love ere thou Love hadst become.

11/7
(after bathing three times)
(On melody specially composed)

Ancient note at Holywell concludes thus: "...and after the hede of the Vyrg-
yne was cut of and touchyd the ground, as we afore have said, sprang up a
welle of spryngyng water largely endurying unto this day, which heleth al
langours and sekenesses as well in men as in bestes, which welle is named
after the name of the Vyrgyne and is called St. Wenefrede's Welle."

DYMA BABELL Y CYFARFOD

Mae yna ryw gilfachau yn y cof
Na wyddys am eu bod, hyd nes y deir
Yn ôl i'w mynedfeydd. Paham y dof
Ar grwydr greddf i'r parthau lle y'm gwneir
Mewn ennyd hynny'r wyf? Pa fagned sydd
Yn tynnu er ein gwaethaf ar ein craidd
A edwyn hen donfeydd colledig ddydd,
A deimla gyffro rhyw doredig wraidd?
O nefoedd wen, pa rym fedd henaidd faen
Na wna ond gorffwys, gorffwys fel yr oedd
Yn dawel yn ei le, yn haen ar haen
O hen gladdedig oriau? Sŵn pa floedd
Sy'n mynnu dod yn ôl ar donnau'r gwynt
A gofyn, "Ble buost ti ar d'ofer hynt?"

16/7

(Y Tabernacl, Caerdydd)

GRADUATION

As days return we shall return no more
To think together or to sit and smile
O'er academic sippings, that restore
The creaking overladen brain awhile.
The moments will pass through these monuments
Without a thought of us, nor shall we know
That as we cross these gates old merriments
Will from fond faces shine with friendship's glow.
Together do we in one parting meet,
By many winds to be now borne along.
What paths henceforth will carry these same feet
That here in order move to Youth's last song?
Dear fading friends, when many dusks have been,
What will this setting sun by then have seen?

18/7

RHIW GOCH AND CARMEL

Beneath this veil there hides an utter force
That utters nought but matters much to some
That passing by have once here fixed the course
Of lengthy vacant hours thenceforth to come.
Beneath this tent is rent the pulling heart
That could see what is seen, that could love well,
And yet, strange unseen Love, here where Thou art
Can no more think with what is seen to dwell.
There is a fire that burns the very soul,
And scorched e'en is the land where some have trod,
And, sister, we perhaps unwisely stroll
In regions densely mingled with our God.
For there are some who come not back again
From this excruciating Bliss of pain.

Rhiw Goch: birthplace of St John Roberts, Benedictine
martyr of the Eucharist. Dolgellau Carmel is nearby.

Pauvre malheureux prêtre

O Saint of God, whose eyes saw as His saw,
Thou wast not made for earth, yet didst it shake,
For Ars meant nought to any heart before,
Yet nations did by storm this village take
And lay thee under siege for but a word,
A sound whereon to found the coming years –
A word, O Father, but a word once heard
From the Beyond whereon thou hadst strange ears.
O! mystery of Choice that dost descend
To crannies of this globe, 'twould seem each age
Traps somewhere some stray rays that
Thou dost send To dullard brains when aiming at the sage.
O Père! though now thou'rt o'er the Stygian sea,
On this day canst thou find some sound for me?

Ô Saint de Dieu, ami de mon enfance,
Vois-tu ce soir la nuit, la nuit profonde
Qui maintenant remplace l'abondance
Qui luisait au matin? Car sur ce monde
Le flot des années coule, et nous reprend
Sans nous demander si notre œuvre est faite.
Et toi, à ce tournant, tu me rapprends
Le chemin de notre aube, où Dieu nous guette.
Ô! grace de l'aurore, viens encore
Me placer dans les traces de ces anges
Dont aujourd'hui j'entends la voix sonore
M'inviter à me joindre à ces phalanges
De petits riens brisés, broyés, morts,
Qui surent retrouver leur premier sort.

4/8

(On specially composed melody)

DEIGRYN

(ar ôl gweld llun Raymond Williams)

Fwyn riant yn y ffydd, a glywi'n awr
Yr anuniongred gri na ddylai ddod
O'r parthau hyn at entrych nefol Wawr
Lle mae dy olwg bellach? Ai di-nod
Yw'r synau bychain oll lle'r ŷm yn troi
Am ryw eiliedyn ar y draethell hon
Ger cefnfor yr eonau na chawn ffoi
Yn hir, cans llanw ddaw ar fechan don?
O dad, a gerddaist ddoe drwy'r dŵr o'm blaen,
A gofi iti unwaith roi dy law,
Ac i'th leferydd dreiddio trwchus faen
Rhyw gell? Yn awr, heb wybod beth a ddaw,
A fedraf ddanfon heresi drwy'r rhod,
Ac erchi am it erchi Awdur Bod?

9/8

TORTURE

Of what is made a pain? How is combined
The sound of this alarm that all must heed?
Of what is made a brain, that has refined
The niceties of utmosts that may plead
Upon an armoured will to give, to give
A moment of consent? Is this one ball
The pocket of the Cosmos where hours live
Within a state of feeling? Is Time all?
Or are there aches æonic o'er the sea
Whence none returns? O Seconds strangely riv'n,
You trickle into hell and ecstasy,
And some cry that no moments more be giv'n.
'Mid cyclic paths where spheres moved in the void,
There was but one where thought with feeling toyed

CRI DE CŒUR
(from Carmel)

There are some sounds that move the earth and melt
The solid mould of Mind. There are some looks
That gaze into our gazing, where is spelt
The meaning of long shelves of unwrit books.
There is in absence presence of a sort
That presence rarely knew, and solitude
The workings of the heat doth well report
To ears attuned awhile to quietude.
We are what we desire, and what we are
Is known when known alone. The sound of need
Is heard when sounds have ceased, and from afar
We hear the echo that sound cannot hear.
For we are all we are when all is gone,
And there is knowing in the lonely one.

A PACT

(I'll have you fluffing up my halo)

When æons have rolled on and here below
We are but letters chiselled on a stone;
When waves of time have lapped the lands we know
And hushed to sleep each nursed and rested bone
That now is stroked and fondled; when the days
That gulp the moments shared and rack those not,
Have in Oblivion dropped from mem'ry's gaze,
And ages have in trickling all forgot;
Then will there be in some dark corner hid
Amid the fields of Light, some chuckle yet
Unheard except by two, for that one bid
The other one old vow not to forget?
And once upon an æon will we see
A little cherub grin shine tidily ?

THERE IS NO CURE

Of all that hurts this is the oldest hurt,
And patient searching no medicament
Has found whereby was bound this speck of dirt
That in its rampant growth has growing bent
To wilting ere much youth was fully grown.
No order this disorder ever tamed,
And though this realm of Chaos be well known
(For that in all e'er written it was named),
There is a hollowness where each stray soul
Has met the great Abyss, and touched the spot
Where many beings were engulfèd whole
By one sharp Pull that pulled to depths so hot
That nothing could be felt beyond the pain
That hacked at each live soul till it was 'twain.

(On melody specially composed)

I THINK *I* DO HAVE A CALL

Wilt thou be wimpled, little one; wilt thou
Be drawn from many gazes that could peep
Yet at this virgin land? Will thy wings now
Be clipped, that all thy dreams may vigil keep
Beside thy silent Lover? And the hours
That, tapping, will rule o'er our severed days,
Will they in Mem'ry's holes let rest some flow'rs
That were once seen and plucked on windswept ways?
O little, little one, within thy breast
The world was safe awhile, and it held all
That was e'er needed by a need at rest,
For cosmic joys are sometimes very small.
O huge Demand, we know 'tis short, we know,
And yet there is long loneliness below.

Awaiting an answer

Within a leaf are folded many days,
And when there is no noise the future lies
In lingering abeyance 'tween forked ways.
Yet there is in the hungering of eyes
That see no message come, familiar void
That its unknowing knows at least as known
And can with undashed dreams still be employed,
For that the flame of Hope is not yet blown.
To know or not to know the very ruth,
Which is the better, when the truth can hurt?
And is there bliss at times in untaught Youth
Worth much Age taught, that naught can e'er revert?
And are we safer with a folly's dream
Than with a wisdom that has lost its gleam?

JUST ONE

The world is less a lonely place
When there is one, but one
To whom the features of one face
Are where a world has shone.

The world is less a lonely place
When there are but two eyes
Whose gaze bears some old healing grace
To one who was unwise.

The world is less a lonely place
When there is but a touch
That bids the heart beat on apace
'Neath pulsings felt as such.

The world is less a lonely place
When there is but a sound
That smooths the lines that worries trace
On temples that oft frowned.

The world is less a lonely place
When there is but a scent
That is recalled in th'interlace
Of limbs that mem'ries lent.

The world is less a lonely place
When there is but a taste
Of presence that did void replace
When two paused in their haste.

The world is less a lonely place
When there is but a friend
Who in the hurry of this race
Had moments yet to spend.

(On melody specially composed)

Touch

To know that there is presence in a hand
And mingled mind in sharing of a heat,
That in the chill of Chaos two can stand
Unharmed, and with a smile great Sadness greet,
That when we seem but specks of cosmic dust
Or ants unknown soon trodden underfoot,
There is a care somewhere for what yet must
Be there for one, just one, that understood –
This is to know that there are many things
Of weight that can weigh less than something small,
So small that imperceptibly it clings
Amid a ruin huge that ruins all.
But this small clinging holds a soul to soul
At touching pores that keep two fragments whole.

THE EIGHTH AGAIN

"Life is but Time; Time life," she said, and thought
How more had gone, without being beckoned on.
The story is but happ'nings somewhere caught
Within a web well weaved, yet still not done,
That in the Cosmos hangs from end to end
And lets small being crawl a little while
Upon the lines of Pattern that they mend
With care and worry hole calm æons smile.
And yet a little time can turn the world
To orbits yet known, untraced; and scared
Is the lost unwatched creature to be hurled
On paths that lead too far from one that cared.
For there is where is one a place for two
To shelter from two lifetimes passing through.

8/9
(in retreat,
Kilnacrott Abbey)

Contemplare, et contemplata aliis tradere

O Master of the vineyard, what are these
White robes that are yet offered to a soul
That could again be plunged in grace, which sees
The small, the great, the greater, and the whole
Within a moment's vision, when the sight
Of what is seen and studied is seen less
Than things not yet beheld in regions bright
That open at the stroke of limbs that bless?
O world beyond the world, can words beget
New angel bands to walk toward thy shore,
And is there use for thought more fruitful yet
Than inward thinking, that packed well its store?
Is there a way, good Lord, that we can walk
Together thought in thought, and of this talk?

10/9
(in retreat, reading the life of St Norbert)

I AM HERE.
WHY LOOK ANY FURTHER?

O little ring of glory made of love,
Look on and on and on and melt the all.
Small particle of essence from above,
In dead of night without a sound a call
From depth of Presence dense removes the earth
From many orbits' centre, and these rays
With which Man's art would point t'ward Godhead's worth
Would seem to point to where must point my days.
O ancient Miracle of ages old
That pondered and that wondered long at this,
Have hominids at times been somewhat bold
Not dreading while oft treading realms of bliss?
And is one hour too long for puzzlement,
When God scarce mastered this experiment?

12/9
(at night, before the monstrance)

God scarce mastered...: Written while reflecting on the video about
Eucharistic miracles, in which the Host sometimes failed to con-
ceal the change.

WHAT NAME WILL YOU TAKE?

And so will this begin to be the end
Of goings forth too often rebegun?
This crooked way that our meanders wend,
Will it seem straight beneath our setting sun?
Can we belong to corners of this earth
When we but long to linger no more here
Where little beings have but little worth,
Unless for one or two who once drew near?
And thou, hid angel that from heaven came,
Wilt thou be lonely in thy starry sky
Made all of Song and Silence? Will a name
That will be quickly shed so quickly die?
And will we ponder when the years have gone
What in two weeks was done and left undone?

12/9
(last night in retreat)

Λέγει αὐτῷ, Ἀκολούθει μοι
(For a clothing at Carmel)

O gentle voice, whose noise is seldom heard,
Voice of my Lord, speak on without a word,
Bid silence heed the echo of a sound
Hid from all ears save hers whom Thou hast found.

Master, speak on: Thy servant listens here
Where Thou art present, where Thy touch is near.
Words are true words when all is left unsaid,
For 'tis in silence that e'n angels tread.

Lord, thou hast called and, calling, Thou dost bid
That one called soul do now as many did
O'er ages vast, now past and yet still seen
In mem'ry's gaze by those who here had been.

Call, call again; I'd follow where here trod
Virgins who felt the treading of their God.
Master, I'd come; I'd come and follow Thee;
Bid words of silence be enough for me.

(On Abide with me)

At the Carmel Gate

O little house of prayer so full of love
Shed not on many things, shed not at all,
'Twould seem to sight below – for sights above
Here every hidden heart to hid realms call –
Thou dost hold 'tween thy walls long hours well sealed
From moments that can rise and fall again
On senses swiftly pierced and slowly healed
Upon this rugged road made of much pain.
O harmless band of angels, how you hurt
The heart that loved too well a part of you . . .
Farewell, fond fledgling that one hour didst skirt
The fringe of very bliss that grew and grew.
Move on to the beyond wherein we are
Not meant for moments that more moments mar.

1/10

WE HERE WELCOME YOUR APPLICATION...

A word unheard but read and said within,
Where many hurting words have knived their place,
Can in a moment cover all the din
Of clamoured Worry, that left not a space
For aught but its own voice – a stroke of sense,
A line of meaning shaped to guide a life
Holds in a fragile pattern forces dense
That traverse eye and brain to depths of strife.
O moment of relief, abide with me
An hour or two, ere more pain bid thee go.
O quietness of Care, I'd feel for thee,
And fondle one last time a face I know.
For I perceive that I'll not handle long
A passing dream to whom two pasts belong.

2/10

BURN THE LETTERS

The words that uttered were from breast to breast
While travelling o'er the page, the pulsèd waves
Of thinking and of feeling that could rest
Immobile in mobility that craves
To reach its journey's end – the little beats
Of early waking love, must they now sleep
An everlasting sleep as these dumb sheets
From every hour to come their secret keep?
O little sibling of a nun, what fun
Unheard again will 'neath thy wimple lie
Far from suspecting ears? The markings done
Upon a long- lost page here one last sigh
Give out ere they e'ermore give out their strength
To cry far 'yond the span of mem'ry's length.

ACCEPTED

What in a word resides, what in a sound,
None knows save one who waited for it long.
What peace can bathe a track, a small path found,
None sees save one who did to night belong.
There is yet hope, for we grope not alone,
But hold the Hand that placed a mark or two,
Enough that we might tread from stone to stone
Along an ancient footpath that it knew.
Farewell, archangel that from Heaven came;
Complain no more of strokings too well felt.
Shine on in thy fond smiling still the same,
For 'tis the gaze that did my winter melt.
Move on to cherub heights, and there abide,
And if I reach there first, I'll for thee hide.

11/10

We are a flashing moment in the day
Of grey unnoticed hours; we are a spot
Upon the æons' charter, where a ray
Did move upon a time and bid it not
Haul on without an interval to gaze
At Yesterday's fond visage; we are here
Upon the page we scribble, and our days
Can sometimes travel far and yet be near.
For we have means whereby we can still hold
A moment of felt holding; we have eyes
That can our looking capture, and things told
To ears that loved to listen can the skies
Yet travel for a while and land again
Upon a little sheet we thought to stain.

Pictures...: "Pictures are important. They capture Time, and we're going out of Time."

HOME

To squeeze, squeeze on until the æons yawn,
To rest within the breast where nestles love,
To lie without a care where bliss was born,
And to stroke on and on one tiny dove
That flew whence I knew not and paused awhile
Upon this rugged track – to hold what held
The meaning of all meanings in a smile
And to behold what all my thought beheld:
This would in very truth be ecstasy
If it were meant to be, if it were all
That was e'er meant to be, for what we see
Is to the Eye that sees us very small.
And there are vistas in the firmament
That know of other kinds of merriment.

18/10
(Caernarfon)

THAT'S THE BOAT THAT'S TAKING MY ALUN AWAY

Within an inch or two there breathes a world
That this great vessel moving into land
Bids for all hours in one brief hour be hurled
Into a distance huge. This little hand
Now fondled one more time, these big, big eyes
Now gazing o'er the sea, this faithful heart
Now tapping its adieu towards the skies
That will henceforth alone link thoughts that part,
Will these still want the touch of wanting, that
Can hence be known but by those touches known
By those who know one other, who know what
Was known when two knew things that were their own?
O presence that here absence dost become,
Was ever Meaning such on lips so dumb?

18/10
(Holyhead)

WAVING

Farewell, sweet phantom, ne'er imagined, ne'er
E'er thought to be a possible of time.
Wave on, wave on and on into the air
Of faint receding years that now must climb
Into the ancient past where once we trod
Together in the wind of mighty things
That were too strong for us, for they were God
O'ershadowing lost fledglings with strange wings.
I hear thee cry across the growing waves
And see the tears that this deep ocean draws,
For there are forces that no mortal braves
And moments where Eternity must pause.
O little shrinking spot, the utterness
Of Being in thee grows now less and less.

MORNING HAS BROKEN

O quietude unruffled, O vast space
Of sanctity awaiting to be filled,
What days, what hours await in this still place
The trickling of our thoughts? O thing unwilled
Of what is part of us, yet wanted well
By what is there, was there 'neath many sighs,
Thou dost redeem lost seconds with a bell
That bids the heart to better things arise.
O nightmare of a dream, say 'tis not so,
That we must start a journey oft begun
And on a day the days of Sisyph know
To be in spending spent with little won.
We are a life in living a mistake,
And learn towards the end the road to take.

19/10

Morning has broken...: Hymn et conventual Mass at the Abbey.

ACCIDENT?

There are some loves that heat in cooling much
And ponder newer gestures that the old
First fondled flame of youth would have thought such
As would have been esteemed a little bold.
There are some shades of meaning that a cup
Can in a moment bear, and there are signs
Of limited affection that move up
Th'excited spine when minds speak unto minds.
There is a mellowing in youthful lust
That is so truly ripe that fulness breaks,
And in the knowledge of an ancient trust
'Twill weather yet a storm or two that shakes.
And yet methinks I could have fondled long,
And for a wrinkled body had a song.

19/10

Accident? – The farm help replied: "The wife hit me with a cup."

AND THERE WAS EVENING...; THE FIRST DAY

To be alone with God, to be alone
With what alone doth last; to be, to be:
This is all being here – being unknown
(Save at the outer front, where some may see
A merriness contrived), unknown to all
Save One who knows it all; unknown, I say,
Save unto Thy Strange ears, O King, whose call
E'en through the din of Pleasure found a way.
O Master, I let go of all not gone
From fondness'grip; I'd have a grasp of things
Not made of what we are, for though there shone
A gentle light that of a greater sings,
I know of some strange God-shaped void within
That will not cease to ache till I walk in.

19/10

LISTEN

There is a silence in this place, so pure
That animals alone dare it defile.
There is serenity of faith that is so sure
That Man walks with his God, and sees Him smile.
There is an unlost childhood in this land
That dares yet to believe what mothers said
In evenings past, long past – that dares to stand
Alone upon this globe that grown men tread.
There is a wisdom in th'unhurried field
That prowess of the head outshone in haste,
And there are technic arts that old wives wield
That would to logic's annals cause distaste.
Yet there are mighty things in muttered sounds
That in a land of magic have no bounds.

DAWN
(before the Blessed Sacrament)

An hour of stillness ere the world awake,
An hour or two of waiting for a sound
Not made of voice, three hours a breath to take
Of angel ether ere begin the round
Of earthy doings that surround the hours
With pulls conflicting splitting what we are
Into the million morsels where our pow'rs
Have been demanded here and channelled far...
A silence to behold, to hold awhile
An energy entire, and consecrate
The looking of the dawn to one soft smile
That could pass unawares, should morn not wait
A virgin moment ere words break upon
The sleeping æons that must call us on.

ROSARY

Thou couldst not trap a blessing, little one,
Or find anointed hands to sanctify
These hard-sought beads of meaning, that now run
'Tween fingers that no more may testify
To truths unsaid, which they could utter well;
Thou couldst not consecrate or call a charm,
But in despair thou didst these beads so tell
That thou didst Heav'n's last rubrics all disarm.
For in thy sorrow thou didst pray for me
Whom thou wouldst nurse no more, and in thy prayer
The floodgates of thy loving were set free
And did great beads of weeping bid fall there
Where now I hold a blessing of a kind
That rarely did a pontiff ever find.

AD MAIORES REDIVIT

Upon this road have many travellers come
And gone to where they are – to where they are
Today as yesterday in their long home
That seemed to them too once so very far
From closely touching minutes that filled all
That clung unto their void; – to where they are
This night as every night that shall e'er fall
And hold an untold dream no dawn can mar.
Where now they are! – O ! voyage quickly made,
And seldom made again by those who go
This mile not made of measure – here is played
The die that we cast once and ne'er more throw.
There moves upon this shore a mystery,
And moments matter an eternity.

1/11
(All Saints)

Ad maiores...: "She went to join the majority." (Our faithful neighbour died today.)

196

A SHOCK

(after hearing about what the Russians were trying to silence)

"And now I plead with you," the statesman said,
"Let not the sceptics squash this story, or
By terror halt its spreading..." – Can the dead
Be so alive to Science that a store
Of facts untapped can by its ears be heard,
Recorded, measured, made to move the hairs
Of doct and placid Reason? Can a word
Be from dumb engines brought that no sound bears?
Inferno of a dream, is this rave Fact
That matters more than Fiction could have thought?
And is there mighty Action in one act
Of gentle passing to the realms of nought?
And are there some now, now, yes even now,
Who know reality we know not how?

Statesman: special counsellor to Norway's Minister of Justice.

The Divine Mercy

There is a place where peace and mercy meet,
Where human kind
The rays of Godhead can in darkness greet
And healing find.
There is a Manhood where Divinity
Looks out to us
From all Eternity.

O stream of light, O beam of ancient grace
Giv'n in this hour
For us, for us who in this tender Face
Behold the Power
That uttered Time, that bid the moments be:
I see this gaze
That waited long for me.

O Master, draw me close to this soft heat
That melts e'en this,
The coldness of the heart where all things meet
Except thy bliss,
And in a smile bid me awhile drink deep
Here where there is
A place for those who weep.

November, 1991
(in retreat, Mellifont)
(On melody specially composed)

Divine Mercy: Written for the opening of the Mercy Shrine at our
Abbey on the 18th of next month.

CISTERCIAN NIGHT

The inner life hangs on the tip of this
Small finger of alarm that calmèd hours
Holds nightly 'fore the eyelids that can miss
The force of thought in Stillness, where the pow'rs
Of Mind are in their virgin strength all free
To hear what comes from list'ning, what alone
Can be perceived, received on bended knee
Where heart and Heart know sounds that are their own.
O Master, I have met Thee here before,
And trembled at thy loving; I have heard
In these thy vigil moments meanings more
Profound than sound can hold when word blunts word.
And I perceive that I must e'er wind this
Until it hurts, if I would feel thy kiss;
That Will must turn this little, little wand
That into being taps this ancient land.

23/11
(in vestition retreat, before dawn,
Mellifont Abbey)

ÉCONOMIE

Désormais que j'écoute ce que disent
Ces voix qui veulent parler; que je sache
Écouter même ce que ces yeux lisent
Sur chaque page sacrée où se cache
Ta douce Voix bâillonnée; que se taise
En mon esprit ce besoin de se faire
Entendre, encor s'entendre, et qu'il Te plaise,
Dieu du secret, de dire en quoi se taire.
Ô! vie intérieure, reste-là,
Là où nous sommes, car pour être vrai,
Il suffit de ne pas vivre au delà
De cette vie d'écoute où tout se tait.
Car beaucoup peut se perdre en quelques sons
Qui obscurcissent souvent l' horizon.

24/11
(in retreat, before dawn)

Your Order is gloriously eucharistic
and eucharistically glorious

'Tis good, 'tis good to be for ever Thine,
To gaze upon Thy throne, and in Thy home
To have my little dwelling, even mine,
Hard by Thy tent, where Thou dost whisper, "Come,
Come often, come e'en closer, come and stay
A lengthy moment here where men come not
For converse with their God upon their way
To regions where much action is forgot."
O Sun whence rays of love now warm this road
That henceforth lies ahead, I would Thee feel,
Thee fondle, handle, and this small abode
E'er with my loving shelter, and oft kneel
Where angels are, where matters of great weight
Can for an unknown matter stand and wait.

24/11
(in retreat)

Your Order...: Pope Pius XI (1932) referred to it as:
gloriose eucharisticum et eucharisitice gloriosum.

CONFITEBOR

The sin that has been great has been so small
That it could not be seen till what it worked
The work of Grace undid. 'Tis sad to fall,
But sadder to have stood when ruin lurked
To bid the solid topple, not in noise,
But in a silence in one vast domain –
For 'tis not mighty sinning that annoys
The Builder of this work, but one deep stain.
The thankless heart is what will thy Heart rend,
O Giver of it all: the soul not giv'n
To waiting for a moment oft to send
A blessing for a blessing of thy Heav'n.
For Grace is stored or lost in this one thing
That made of one giv'n much a wanderling.

25/11
(at dawn, in retreat)

Age quod agis

To live here in the now of Thy command,
To do well this one thing that is here done;
To be where Thou this hour dost bid me stand,
And leave the work of other hours undone –
This is to rule eternity by one,
One passing lasting moment caught in flight;
For 'tis in dropping others that is won
The mastery of this strange speck of light.
Tomorrow never was and ne'er shall be,
Nor shall a yesterday be doctored here,
But there are many moments close to me,
And marred or modelled years are very near.
O sacrament of moments, one alone
I'll take to make æonic grace my own.

25/11
(in retreat)

Age quod agis: "Do what you are doing". (Written in retreat while
meditating on advice in Manual for Novices: "Perform each in-
dividual action as though it were the only thing you have to do;
for that particular action alone is in your power at the time of its
execution. Do not permit your actions, any more than your days,
to interfere with one another.")

KIND WORDS ARE THE MUSIC OF THE WORLD

A being made of love to all that come
Within its magic rays, always the same,
Always a friend where friend can find a home,
An overtone borne by a little name:
This is to be alive, and to be there
In that small corner of the universe
Where we were set a while, a weight to share
With one or two who wanted to converse.
For there are two great forces in the earth
That can both heal and harm, that can do all
That need be done to make one life of worth:
The one is Silence; th'other Sound withal,
And there can be a presence in a soul
That in soft glowing made some being whole.

25/11
(in retreat)

Kind words...: Words of the great Oratorian, Fr William Faber.

FAMILIAR

O! Peace of Cîteaux, now so very near
And yet so far away for evermore,
Is there no way to hold these hours so dear
That were one hour dropped hurriedly before?
O ancient magic calling from afar!
Can we e'er cease to be what we were made?
And though we wander 'neath a new-found star,
Does youth's first loving all so quickly fade?
O tears of things! I cannot not be this
At least within, where there is room to be
Trapped in the sanctum of unclamoured bliss
Where silence bore enough to nurture me.
We need not cease to be so utterly
The only thing that we could ever be.

26/11
(in retreat)

Tout

Louange de cette gloire qui me dit:
«Viens, entre par ici, et sers-Moi bien
Là où mes voies te mènent», – oui, ainsi,
Ainsi je serai, car ce petit lien
De mince étoffe fait, me tire au ciel
Qui n'est pas loin d'ici, car ces nuées
Qui montent souvent devant cet autel
Contient des ailes cachées, embaumées.
Ô Gloire! fais du moins que maintenant
Je sois à Toi, pour Toi, que ce regard
Qui m'a aimé, me garde à mon Amant,
Et que mon cœur verse une fois son nard.
Car cette gloire a souvent appelé,
Et cet amour est ici mal aimé.

9/12
(after taking the habit, and also the Pioneer pledge)

IL NUOVO OROLOGIO
(nella cappella dell'adorazione)

Rumore della notte, sempre qui
Vicino al Silenzioso, che
Mi guarda e mi mormora così
Senz'altra voce che le suppliche
Del Cuore che è là; battito mai
Udito nel passato qui, perché,
Perché venirci? Ahimè, tu hai
La forza per le gravi cariche!
Non odo più la solitudine
Di questa veglia nell'oscurità,
Ma forse la beatitudine
Si cela ora dove palpita
Il tuo cuore ferreo, che sa
L'Omega dell'antica Verità.

14/2/92

LA VERGINE DELLA RIVELAZIONE
(Tre Fontane, il 12 aprile 1947)

È dunque vera, questa verità
Che non volevo credere, perché
Non era scritta né sentita, là,
– Almeno alle mie orecchie, –
Nel testo sacro dove solo fu
Udita quella Voce che non ha
Né bocca né parola? Gioventù!
Che paradiso la semplicità!
La Vergine che non veniva mai
Sull'orizzonte del credente, che
Sapeva tutto bene, qui ormai
M'insegna delle strane pratiche.
Non so però se anche l'estasi
Sa ben illuminar i lucidi.

4/4

SHE STOOD ABOVE US ON A CLOUD

Obscurity where brightness hid us all
That marched in this dark Calm! We did hold on
To something in the air, and we heard fall
A curtain made of Mystery whereon
Some angel feet did patter, yet knew not
That 'twas their Queen that walked the air that stirred
Above our flick'ring Aves. Little spot
Of blessing on the globe – to think, 'twas heard –
This very name was uttered in the skies
That mapped e'en my mad shufflings: 'twas pronounced
By Her who in the heavens softly cries –
"I'd come to Kilnacrott" was mused, announced,
And happened in the dead of this long night:
This was the jerk that blurred my weeping sight.

What is the matter shattering the law
Of order on this border of the world?
What cometh hither from the æons' shore
In ill-definèd particles so hurled
From realms untapped, whose untrapped pow'rs bemuse
The itching heads of scholars? What are these
Great tranquil blobs of Evidence that use
Our simple toys to chuckle and to tease?
O wand'ring Myth, that comest once again
Across this page of thinking where no thought
Can linger long within the out-thought brain,
Thy spark oft alleluias here hath wrought.
And there is beauty in antiquity
So old that it can print eternity.

20/4
(Easter Monday)

One of the negatives...: Photographer's comment on returning print
of apparition to member of our Community.

TRUGAREDD

Mae yma fan lle'r erys ôl Ei draed
Ar lwybrau Dyn,
Ac yn Ei gwpan Ef mae dafnau Gwaed
A wnaed yn wir
At archoll y colledig a fu ffôl
Yn troi a throi
Cyn dychwel yma'n ôl.

Mae yma awr lle daw'r holl oriau maith
Yn eiddo in,
Ac ym munudau'r rhannu hwn fe ddaeth
Drwy ddwyfol Win
Yr hyn sydd hen yn newydd, gan mai Ef
A drefnodd hwn
O ryfedd neithior Nef.

Ac y mae yma heddiw bethau cudd
Na welwn ni,
Cans o gylch rhaniad hwn adenydd sydd
Heb sain na si
Yn troedio ar gymylau thus rhy bêr
I ni eu gweld,
Cans dyma ôl Duw Nêr.

(On melody composed for "The Divine Mercy")

SUNRISE OVER MELLERAY

Is this a miracle that moves
And moves and moves again with dizzy spin
O'er this strange spot? And is it this that proves
The truth that I long knew to be within
Soft beckoning to give my all to this
Small particle of burning? Sacred Host,
In hiding earth's own light, art thou from Bliss
Here sent and meant to show what burneth most?
And that Our Mother should shed tears here seen,
All at the frigid eating of her Sun,
And bid not hither come where we have been,
But next be all at Kilnacrott as one –
This means more than e'er meaning can enfold,
For I perceive that burning hands me hold.

17/5

KEEPING WATCH
(before the Monstrance, 2-3 a.m., Ascension)

O! sacred hour, wherein the all is still,
When even Thought thinks not, but listens well,
When wanting fills no more the worried will
And noise-machines withhold awhile their yell:
I hear the trickle of a truth where now
Two hearts exchange a gaze, where seeing means
The touching of a ray, and where somehow
I see the sight of many ancient scenes.
For I am here alone where saints have trod
Into the angel-light, and what I hear
Was heard by all who came, for this my God
Stands in the realm of Silence, oddly near.
For little eyes peep through the dreaming air
Across the skies of Time at what gleams there.

I FELT A TINGLING

O touch! O coupling of the earth and sky
In word and sound intense with meaning sent
Into the silent void, high, high on high
Where guesses softly probe! O utt'rance meant
With every fibre of the brain! O plea
Of one last pause to want and want
A hearing 'hind the clouds! To wait and be
With Being joining hands is here to pant
Upon a moment's gamble where our all
Pulls every rope of promise, knowing not
If Will Divine move at a beck so small
As this that strokes one hidden pain forgot –
And to hear that 'twas heard, this is too much
To hold within the tingle of a touch.

I'M GOING IN ON OUR LADY OF MOUNT CARMEL

Will those big eyes peep out upon the world
That they awhile did warm, from cloistered grille,
And will that tiny planet now be hurled
Into a starlit orbit t'ward a Will
That strangely pulled apart two meteors
Allowed once to collide? Will that small heart
Still pat upon the moments that it stores
Alone where hours unborn once wept to start?
O little thing that walked upon this earth
With feet well-known and fondled; tiny breast,
That once didst shield a child 'neath sweetest mirth
Made of maternal loving, wilt thou rest
Now far away from this receding dream
That carries yet a morsel of thy beam?

Laus Gloriæ
(St Norbert)

O Saint of God, who walked this way
On which the feet of many trod,
We follow here an ancient ray:
We travel in the light of God.

To glory you have led this throng
Of brethren now in raiment clad
Of purest white, whose triumph song
Bids us who follow here be glad.

O Master, we have heard your call
And would walk on, for to this praise
Of Majesty we will give all,
And hallow here on earth our days.

The incense of a hidden cloud
Of witnesses, who at the Throne
Fall now in silent praise too loud
For us to hear, o'er us has gone.

And so, good Master, stretch your hand,
And beckon t'ward this quire, where sound
Is made to move where angels stand,
And is to endless Beauty bound.

6/6

(On specially composed melody)

THE VIGIL

O night of nights, that held such hours of light!
We little knew what knowledge would here flow
In wave on wave of Grace, where hidden sight
Espied what nought sees save in Vision's glow.
'Twas seen, this region dark, not once or twice,
But thrice since eve, and once, yes, 'twas in me.
And this thy sharpened gaze a heart of ice
Did melt, sweet sister, 'neath these rays that see.
For thou didst utter things that only One
Had ever known, and to know this small thing
Means much, means very much to one alone,
For now I know that these two marks must cling
To little hands of healing that can touch
A body full of soul that hurts too much.

6-7/6

(Pentecost)

Thrice: the miracle of the sun, the apparition to Patricia, and Sr
Monica's vision and discernment.

I SAW...

O Mother of my Lord, to know that thou
Dost hold me thus, and watch me with such love;
That this small mangled being can somehow
Be as a jewel seen by one above
The cherubim and seraphim in light —
That thou, my fairest Queen, shouldst in thy hand
Be seen to hold me thus, in Vision's sight,
And with a smile to gaze from yonder height:
This could but melt the thickly frozen years
Of wand'ring, wond'ring waste; yet ' tis not all:
Thou hast, sweet, gentlest Mother, wiped my tears
For ever by this last one word so small
Yet huge within my heart, for thou, 'twas said,
Hast for me yet a marvel in thy head.

9/9
(St Columcille's day,
reflecting on Sr Monica's message)

THIS IS THE LAST TIME YOU'LL SEE ME WITH HAIR

Goodbye, my cherub, travel to the skies
That hold our morrows where no sorrows lie,
Where sadness blurs no more the sparkling eyes
That once could read a soul and mark a sigh
Writ in a passing wrinkle... Fare thee well,
Imagination's guest, miss not thy cloud,
Let these two oft-stroked feet tip t'ward the bell
That will their once craved patter now enshroud.
O rending of a world! It is not true!
I loved a ray of Godhead, and thought not
That 'twould e'er come to this. I knew! I knew
What 'twas to hold the heavens in a spot.
And now I see a spot grow e'er so small
And hear this heaven's Author homeward call.

13/6
(at the quay, Dun Laoghaire)

FFRIND

Mae yn ein bod fodolaeth nad yw'n rhan
Ohonom ni; mae yno fwlch o fod
A'n gwna am byth yn dila ac yn wan
Hyd nes y dêl yn un â'r unig nod
Y'i crewyd er ei chyfer. Yma'r ⊠m
Yn teithio unigeddau'r Cosmos hen,
Ac eto mi a wn, am awr fe fûm
Yng nghwmni rhyw belydryn bach o wên:
Yn gwmni i ryw gwmni ar y daith
Fe gefais gongl o'r bydysawd hwn
Yn glyd ymhlith yr eangderau maith
Na chlywent swn fy nghri na maint fy mhwn.
Ond mi a wn wrth ddweud ffarwèl i hon
Mai at Un mwy y teithiai dros y don.

19/6

THE SIGN IN THE SKY

I see the hand that handled even me
With care enough to bring me unto this
Strange vision in the night – I see! I see
The palm and thumb of th'Architect of Bliss Curve
in one sign of love o'er this that now
Becomes this island's map. I hear the sound
Of Heav'ns own tongue, to which mute myriads bow
That now some other utterance have found.
O hand of care, to see thee there, just there
With these mine eyes, that could have stopped to gaze
At what thou once did give, for 'twas so fair...
I now can rest to know here 'mid Night's daze
I have a friend at th'end of this strange way
That brought me back to Erin's ancient day.

21/6
(longest day, Melleray)

Erin's ancient day...: I left Ireland on the eve of the longest day, 1986.

ODOUR

A little member in th'anatomy
Of human kind, so small, yet holding all,
Can carry many things from Thee to me,
O Potter of the earth, for oft the call
Of memory of things and persons sweet
Did of a sudden cry through waves of air
That bade another with this other meet
Upon the oneness of what hovered there.
And yet, though well I knew how sweet the sound
Of ling'ring moments in a perfume touch
Wherein a particle had once been found
Of keenly scented bliss, that mattered much,
I ne'er thought that the matter of a rose
Grown by my Queen would fondle too this nose.

24/6
(reflecting on Kilnacrott vigil)

Odour: The miraculous perfume came every time we waved the
blessed white handkerchiefs, singing Ave...

JESUS!
(Miracle after miracle at the healing
session at the Abbey)

A child like children all, save that the voice
Of this world's singing never reached his ears;
A child whose lips made never known the choice
Of little morsels that might thrill the years
Of early dreams; a child that walked within
A world all, all his own, where none could roam,
For that in this sealed corner not a din
Or echo of this earth e'er found a home:
This little thing of suff'ring suffered all
To pass him by unheard, unanswered – nay,
Ununderstood till he stood 'neath this call
Of heavy Prayer wherein upon a day
A noise came through his ears, and to his tongue
A sermon of a word that stunned this throng.

Jesus! – The first word pronounced by the child.

ANTHONY

There are in little beings heavy things
At work where Heaven moves; there are wee hearts
That hold a portion vast where hidden wings
Protect a seedling grace, for in it starts
The dawn of many morrows born to be
A blessing on the earth. O little soul
So full of utter loving! Thus to see
Thee snore 'fore thy sweet Master made us whole.
For thou dost teach us, little one asleep,
What 'tis to contemplate without much thought
For method and device, for thou dost peep
With this thy twinkle 'yond what tomes have taught .
And there is in thy yawn a merriness
That bids this monstrance stoop in gentleness.

CARMEL

Farewell, my bride; I give thee to my King
To be His lawful queen, for thou must reign
'Mid seraphs, for thou art where cherubs sing,
And dost our weekly watch this night maintain
Not in thy rovings as of yore, but now
Upon thy veilèd knees where others kneel
In odour of soft prayer, and dost there bow
At our own rhythm, for I now thee feel.
O sister, sweetest heart, it was for this
That we did pant together for a while,
And we did know the littleness of bliss
Beside its Fount, who waited with a smile.
For though these bars enclose thee, little one,
I do not grieve that He thy hand hath won.

16/7

SATAN

We move beneath a star that fell of yore
And in its falling heaved a hell of woe
Into the cosmic spheres. The light before
That shone, outshone the seraphs here did grow
Into a burning envy that smites all
That smacks of damnèd glory, and there lies
E'en o'er the bed of innocence a call
To come this occult way and tame the skies.
O little child, art thou a saint so soon
When others have spent ages at the task,
That thou shouldst merit this unwanted boon
Of visits all infernal, and shouldst ask
With nonchalance unnerving things that mean
That thy twelve virgin years grate th'æons' spleen?

Satan: After a vow (never to have anything to do with him), the picture of the Sacred Heart was inexplicably smashed and a note was found at the head of Anthony's bed, written in satanic script: NEVER SAY THAT AGAIN!

THE WEATHER

Is there a tap in Heaven that can turn
So quickly with a nod? Is there a touch
That we and our art's meddling cannot learn
E'en though we sniff deep causes and know much
Of triggers and of links – e'en though we trap
The rules that planted seem upon the globe
And track the root of every chance and hap
That well-peeled eyes observe and duly probe?
Sweet maiden, mighty Mother of this world,
Dost thou upon an æon like to smile
Sometimes and grin betimes to see truths hurled
Into the void that hatched them, and awhile
To mutter some sweet utterance of love,
Enough to bid thy Master Chaos move?

12/7
(ruminating over the way the rain cleared immediately when Fr
Prior requested this publicly of Our Lady at the healing time)

Ubi caritas

There are too many mutterings ill said,
Unmeant, unheard on high, where interest
Need ne'er be giv'n when here our milling head
Is unto every thought save one a nest –
The very thought that need be all there is
Within one little moment richly packed,
A moment fully filled with time all His
Wherein the yearns are on a few sounds stacked.
We have with gentle candles spread a fire
And with sweet virgin voices many choirs
Outsung with these few notes, for from the mire
Of stopwatched Haste we climbed to where respires
The muddled soul made whole by one small touch
Of meaning fully meant where sounds mean much.

21/7
(morning after first Taizé prayer meeting)

Nine

A little man, an adult all at play
With things for bigger heads – a world at one
With heav'n and earth unrent, unparted – nay,
A world of thought untaught by anyone
But this well tutored brain that ticks within,
Where walks a living life as much a home
Of knowing and of sense as lives akin
To knowing many things and sensing some.
Could we behold an old man on his knees
With homeliness like this with mystic art,
And did the full-grown mind grow to this ease
Of gazing, or e'er reach where siblings start?
And in this wanting to do all, give all,
I know that greatness can be very small.

28/7
(after working and praying with
Peter and David, altar boys)

DEPTH

The mastery of speech is in the ear,
And th'ear itself must listen doubly well
To what is very far while very near
The one who waits, for rarely do we tell
What matters to a noise, but poised an hour
Between a hidden past and something new
Made of two knowing hearts, we can in pow'r
Make utterance vibrate if sounds be few.
For I perceive that many, many things
Moved not from depth to depth – that I have heard,
And never heard a thing – for on the wings
Of sound there flies at times an unsaid word,
And we mean well, no doubt, with these two jaws,
Yet meaning often lies within a pause.

31/7
(studying spiritual direction)

SOMEWHERE

There are so many grains of soul afloat
Somewhere, somewhere;
So many pages someone never wrote
Somewhere, somewhere.
There are amid the æons memories
That travel with their load of histories,
And there are scenes long seen that some eye sees
Somewhere.

For there were many ere a word was known
Somewhere, somewhere,
And meanings crossed the air ere sounds were shown
Somewhere, somewhere,
And there was feeling in the heart of Man
Who walked this ground before the ages ran
Their cosmic course from morn to eve's full span
Somewhere.

And many dawns have passed beneath the waves
Somewhere, somewhere;
Across the Stygian flood a tempest raves
Somewhere, somewhere,
For in the ages' memory an hour
Hurts on a little longer, for the pow'r
Of meanings can be felt in sorrow dour
Somewhere.

And yesterday lives on where morrows fade
Somewhere, somewhere
And many moments are with moment weighed
Somewhere, somewhere,
For even though we travel many miles
And seem to matter little here at whiles,
There linger yet some dimmed, forgotten smiles
Somewhere.

2/8
(on returning from megalithic
graves near the Abbey)

(On specially composed melody)

TELL NO ONE

A little more and no more will there be
A time for idling, or a time for this
Or that or th'other act, for History,
It seems, now happens, and henceforth our bliss
Or unrestrainèd pain will our mind's eye
With meaning understood here duly fill.
A warning of a warning that draws nigh
Has reached our eyes and bids us tarry still.
This has been heard before, but not so well,
For now we know of what it shall be made:
Seven minutes whole the very gates of Hell
Will yawn to welcome all who walk this glade.
For every man will glimpse, see utterly,
Of what he is and was the verity.

4/8

Tell no one...: I was to tell only the Prior.

St Augustine

August and glorious ponderer, unseen
Yet heard through Christendom from age to age,
Could e'er thy quill have known what shapes would mean,
What strength of voice it left upon the page?

O hidden face, untraced by any man,
We gaze upon thee through the memory
Of characters that hold what thinking can
Pass through the veins of copied history.

O wielder of the pen that moved the world,
O little head that thought the thoughts of all,
Teach us to feel the moving of a word,
To hear the echo of a sound so small.

For thou didst write and in the height of thought
Didst pause to cause a tremor that would stir
The heart of oft a traveller here caught
Where waves of moving meaning yet occur.

And from the grave of long antiquity
Thy silent hand yet steers our wayward limbs,
And there is in a sound eternity,
For thou hast traced a glory no age dims.

(On specially composed melody)

CLOSE

This is the whisper I have heard before,
But in its sound I have at last found peace:
I know, know well, who 'tis hid by this door
Who waits till I have come and bids all cease
Of action save this one: heed, listen, hark
Through all the pores of thinking – herein is
The resonance of silence, and the dark
Is where alone He has room to be His.
O Master, I have heard a something pull;
Veiled Lover, I have felt a glance here cast.
O Tent by cherubs watched! O air so full –
This, this, and only this, I know at last,
Is what I am being called to do e'ermore:
To watch, watch well, watch ever this strange door.

SORRY

Tis odd what can be found beneath the skin
Of roughness untoward. There is yet grace
In some charred corner lying deep within
The heart that in its beating shapes the face,
And where there is oft sinning there yet gleams
From trammelled Conscience something hugely small
That hurts to think of hurting, and where streams
Of cursings flow some blest thoughts faintly call.
For we know well that we are too well known
To be long out of sight, and night rests ill
Upon a rest ill-gained, and when alone
A man is what he is if he is still.
And there are many things that we need not
Bring to the night when one word all forgot.

Mourir d'amour

A petal, but a petal, is but naught,
Knows naught, says naught, and is as soon forgot
As ere it came to bloom, for ne'er a thought
Could cross its unmade mind, and yet this spot
Of colour aromatic hath borne all
E'er held by oft a heart: a molecule
Of matter dumb hath borne the weighty call
Of Wanting in this wilting pellicule.
And, little flow'r of Carmel, now 'twould seem
That thy fond Bridegroom hath here found a way
Of saying whither hence must move Love's beam,
For though there is no feeling in our day,
I know of knowing in th'unwedded night
That is made all of gazing without sight.

A petal...: On the day of Thérèse's death a shower of roses fell from
the sky over Lisieux. A small boy managed to salvage part of one.
He is now an old priest in Northern Ireland, and gave two petals
to Anthony, who gave one to me. The same miracle happened re-
cently in Ireland, but in connection with Our Lady of Guadalupe.
Rose-petals descended when the massive pro-life march passed
the Dáil, at its junction with the Masonic Lodge.

KINDNESS

There are some beings all of giving made,
And on this land of Erin failings great
Must needs against such weighty acts be weighed,
For good on earth with good is repaid late
Where eye sees not the hand yet reaching deep
In search of that last mite, where ear hears not
The song of angel heads that gently peep
With burning gaze at earnings thus forgot.
We need not do a thing in this domain
Of duty overdone, yet some do more
And more and more, and when 'tis done, again
They dip, 'twould seem, into th'unshrunken store,
For I have heard that Godhead hath oft found
Means of o'ertaking Womanhood's last bound.

RELATIONSHIP

We chatter and we natter lest we seem
Too hurried e'en to care – for Haste burns all
And wastes the passing friendship of a gleam
Of kindliness hid in a morning call –
And as we talk we smile a while and say
What left unsaid would not have changed the sky,
And thus oft little noises cram the day
While sighs unheard heave on and pass us by.
For we are ghosts that look without a gaze
And hurry for we worry lest we pause
Upon a pain, and thus no true flesh stays
To hear the reason or to know the cause.
And it can be that friend can breathe with friend,
And never know of friendship to the end.

THE MORE HE SAW, THE LESS HE SPOKE
(Abbot's words)

Receiving is the all of uttering
The very word, the only word to hit
The point exact, and in much cluttering
Of th'air that bears the waves we often sit
Hard by the naked truth and see it not
Because we know not now to contemplate,
How to behold and hold a sound forgot,
Or how to let an echo resonate.
We are all full of mutterings meant well,
But view not many meanings ere we fire
Our shots into the void, for no sounds dwell
For long where noises throng e'en talks entire.
For talking is with th'eye and th'ear best done,
And with a wait we can bait any one.

JE T'EMBRASSE

How many souls now wander upon earth
Amid so many others, yet alone –
Alone with all the loneliness of birth
Unborn within the body none did own,
Alone with all the heavy weight of mind
Uncarried by another, and with care
All worried by one breast, which did not find
A mouth to suckle 'neath its beauty bare.
O sisters long unwed, shed on your tears
Of molten Wanting where no eye can see,
And utter 'tween the lines what no one hears,
Save one perhaps who knew what 'twas to be
Unable to trust all to any one,
For there are many islands 'neath the sun.

There is an order in this entropy
Of happenings unravelling the hours,
And o'er our heads some ancient canopy
Is stretched, for we are watched by gazing pow'rs
That peeped throughout the night of æons old
At this small spot of Time we fill awhile
With our precisions, our decisions bold,
At which the Ancient Days look with a smile.
There is a providence of things, there is
A knowing and a showing of the way,
Not by oft noises verbal, for 'tis His
To happen, and to utter thus the day,
And we are led, led on by tiny things,
While hap is not the all of happenings.

POSTULANT

(Samuel from Coventry)

Come in and rest awhile, cher frère, come in,
For there is room within my heart for one,
Just one with whom to talk, for oft the din
Of many accents strange and much work done
Upon an alien soil leaves one alone
In company of brethren, and the scene
Unchanging in the cloister leaves its own
A wanderer where memories had been.
Come in, I say, for there is yet a home
Upon this lonely shore, upon this isle,
For some who on lost continents did roam
And paused to listen for a little while
To echoes of a past, a distant past,
That through the storm bid two strays anchor cast.

ADORATION CHAPEL

What prayers, what thoughts have travelled through the air
Between these walls that hold this little space!
How many unheard yearns have reached Thee there,
Hid Master, in this hidden meeting place?
And as the world sleeps on and eyelids seal
The dreams of many souls, and bodies hold
The ecstasy of night, what Presence real
Hath reached out to some hearts that Thee'd enfold?
For as we vigil keep upon the shore
Of living, many things are happening,
And by the hour the deaths and births of more
Migrating souls new stars are wakening.
And some but suffer, and but die and die,
And some but wonder why day passed them by.

16/8
(Dawn, during Somalia famine)

TESTIMONY

So there is more to this than mind and thought,
And words that scratch the ears and then move on:
It seems that to this place some truths unsought
Have found their way, and these lay weight upon
A passing word about a passing guest
Said by a little boy upon a day,
For naughtiness could not have dreamt or guessed
A means to make the heavens drop this way.
Another's word, and yet another's word
About a sudden weight that tilted all,
And at that very spot where we had heard
That something, some One strange did us befall –
This can but carry weight, for weight like this
Is carried normally in realms of bliss.

Testimony...: Prior's account: two bearers who knew nothing of apparition had felt the statue become unbearably heavy at the very spot. Fr Prior also spoke of the direct answer given at Medjugorje regarding the question of the Divine Mercy shrine.

GUIDED

To know that we are in the Will Divine,
That we are turning with the cogs and wheels
Of vast gradated Order, that the whine
Of happenings engaged in Fact reveals
The Act of one deep Thinker – this, and this
Alone can make to resonate again
The song of Earth within the depths that miss
Harmonics of lost joys none can regain.
For we were happy in the simpleness
Of yeses all untied, and to return
To Thee and Thee alone with th'emptiness
That can alone be filled – this is to learn
The meaning of the world, for here we are
The flotsam of a moment from afar.

TWO CHILDREN HOLDING HANDS

Why is it that the hand says more than all
The words that fill the air, and that a child
Can hold another child with links so small
That will yet bond two lives hence where once smiled
The sun of rising warmth, and why do we
When all is said and done do nothing more
Than hold a being by these pores that see
'Neath wrinkled skin the soul that learned this lore?
For there is in a touch much hiddenness
Of understanding grasped, and claspèd limbs
Are bridges whereon pass in gentleness
The moving things that memory ne'er dims.
For we are said when all our meanings stand
Within the grasp of but a clasping hand.

MERCY

I am too old to cry, and yet this word
That came unsought this way from far beyond
The realm of human sound – this message heard
By faculties empow'red by some strange wand
That hands and lips unseen delight to wield –
This bit of earth-bound truth has run me through,
And I have no defence that can me shield
Against the pow'r of joy in something true.
I had not heard of this small clod of earth,
And had e'en less thought of a stake therein,
But now at last I know where came to birth
The puzzling letter that bid enter in.
For this is to be huge, this little place,
And I was followed by a tender Face.

THE VISION

There was once long ago a saintly priest
Who saw beyond the moment and beheld
A mighty boat assailed by vessels least
In size yet most in numbered force, that held
Its sailing under fire, and suddenly
Shot down the one that struggled at the helm,
But killed him not till one rose openly
And with a bullet did all overwhelm.
Then he did see another quickly rise
And take the pontiff's place, and he was shown
Two pillars in the seas set by the skies,
And 'tween the two alone he'd steer his own.
And these two same colossi here now stand
On this our tiny shred of salvaged land.

The vision...: St John Bosco saw it all. The two pillars were the Eucharist and the Blessed Virgin.

LATE EVENING AT KILNACROTT

This is a home from home for many souls,
A hearth where many winter nights we warm,
A stopping-place where oft a pilgrim strolls
On his long homeward journey through the storm.
This is a little land where Heaven dwells,
And people know it well, for still they come
'Neath beating rain, though summoned by no bells
Save th'inner call of coming somehow home.
And through the dark the candles burn, burn on
By statue and by veil, and by this Thing
That hosts an angel throng, and saints have gone
With drunks to meet at these same steps their King.
For there is something strange about this place,
And earthlings seem to huddle round its grace.

A STICK... A BENT KNIFE...

So this is true, the very thing we heard,
That there is to be soon a pause in time!
O Mother of my Lord, this little word
That this child could not find, but only mime –
A sickle – this says all that can be said,
Nay, it says more in that 'twas seen to be
Held in the hand of one with skull for head
And bones for limbs and ribs stretched haggardly.
That other small eyes saw, and that the sight
But echoes what was heard, this can but mean
That what hath reached our ears upon this night
Must soon reach this small globe where Man hath been
A child too long, for now the song is o'er,
And earth will see what ne'er was seen before.

23/8
(Melleray)

Beautiful!

This was a loving gesture, this was love
All thine, yes, Mother Mary, thus to dance
And shine and glisten as the moon above,
As though to cast toward me one fond glance
While using others' eyes, for though I see
No vision in the night, I now know well
That thou dost watch me hard, for 'twas for thee
That I did for thy people these beads tell.
O! telling of a thought, all nought until
Thus parted from the breast and laid to rest
Within the breasts of all who thus did fill
The dark with one small spark of musing blest!
To think that we did all think one same thought
That tickled thee enough to bid thee sport!

23/8
(all night vigil,
Mount Melleray)

Transistor

I turned a switch today which moved the world
Away from here and hither brought the sound
Of darkness, and at one jerk Earth was hurled
Into a distant orbit, for I found
A space wherein to send a thought my own,
Unguided by another from afar,
And to be on this planet once alone,
Beyond the field of some obtruding star.
O! fog of many sounds that clogs the air
We breathe with wheezing soul, what means the need
That some have to do all but stand and stare
Into the Void and for a moment heed
The echoes of the depths that are too shy
With all the pow'r of this small switch to vie?

ALL IS TRUE

And so it seems we have but little time,
And that the words here giv'n are meant for us,
That there is in Creation some soft rhyme
That patters out our measured moments thus
As set e'er in the symphony of days
That could but be, for that Earth chose this course
And that we stand where part our forking ways
While we must yield and bend to Love's great force.
We did yield once before to this strange thing,
But now 'tis 'neath changed visage that it comes
To heal us with a wound, yet one small wing
Is left to these our thoughts, for distant homes
Can by our angels guardian be regained,
And when all cracks Love's gleam will have remained.

All is true...: "All that has been said at Melleray is true... But we will be able to communicate through our guardian angels." Such were the words of the good priest who welcomed the pilgrims at the grotto.

To Our Lady of Kilnacrott,
the Mother of Mercy

We greet thee, Mother Mary, in this place
Where grace and mercy meet, for thou alone
Didst for long gaze into the tender Face
In which th'Eternal's eyes in Time were known.

We greet thee, Mother Mary, on this day
That we have kept for thee, for in this age
Thou hast become a pilgrim on this way
We tread as o'er our head strange forces rage.

We greet thee, Mother Mary, in this night
Where human kind walks all alone astray,
For in the deep'ning dark thy gentle light
And hand outstretched our fears can best allay.

For thou art, Mother Mary, one of us,
And thou dost stand at times upon this shore
Of passing æons, as if meaning thus
To cast a mother's gaze as once before.

(On specially composed melody)

PARKMINSTER CLOSED?

Thou hadst foreseen this day, O Ancient Dawn
That rose before all time; Thou didst but smile
To see me struggle in my tears that morn
That bid me cast aside the robe and style
Of living that I loved: thou couldst read all
The headings of the book that I now end
Ere e'er my mother's eyes did kindly fall
Upon this virgin tome some stall did vend.
And Thou dost know, hid Master, hidden things
That hurt e'en Thy vast gaze, for word on word
From yonder Realm comes hither, and here clings,
For now too many morrows have been heard.
And I behold in holding volumes thus
The pattern of a thoughtwave thinking us.

Parkminster...: In fact the rumour was untrue, but Sélignac itself
was eventually closed.

MESSAGE

To know! To know! At last to know the way
That should be trod, that God Himself hath known –
This is to know of joy, for on this day
A word was heard that hath a whole life shown –
Nay, two whole lives, for thou too, little one,
Wast told what plan the Heavens hold for thee
'Neath long and wimpled hours. And now 'tis done,
The signing of the page that bids thee flee:
For through a tiny child to whom a Queen
Comes oft and with soft accent gives reply,
The vistas of the Godhead have been seen,
And now at last one tranquil heart can sigh
And ponder that our wanderings are o'er,
And that an ancient unction waits e'ermore.

25/10
(applying for vows)

Message: from Heaven, through a privileged child.

HEAVEN'S ANSWER CONCERNING TWO SUICIDES

Somewhere there is a pain that no one knows,
And e'en as I now write a world beyond
The grasp of rhyme fills all the time that flows
On, on and on in trickles that no bond
But History confines to Evermore,
For that the moments writ were stamped for aye
Upon the deep-blotched soul that roamed before
Within the realm of lasting Yea and Nay.
Somewhere there is a sorrow that is long,
But not as long as Ever, and 'twould seem
That in this word was heard a sigh so strong
That it brought to tartaric depths a gleam
Hid in a drop of Blood, a little drop,
Big, big enough to make the æons stop.

Answer: "He is lost. Evil had got hold of him. She is in the deepest level of Purgatory, and needs forty Eternal Fathers to get out of there."

PREPARING FOR VOWS
(and acquiring a new breviary)

To punctuate the moments of the world
With ancient thinking thought and thought again
In placid prayer while onward we are hurled
To happenings of things – and to refrain
From letting things but happen, through being borne
By these refrains and echoes of a past
That lingers in each eve and dawn and morn
And night and noon at which we anchor cast –
This is to wait upon the sound of hours
Until their meaning comes, this is to be
Upon the bridge of seconds where the pow'rs
Of Coming and E'er Gone can look to see
Where all is at upon this little ball
Whose spinning slows with one page's agèd call.

HEAT

To know that we are heard when we but cry
Above the noise of pain into the night;
To know that there is movement in a sigh
That travels to a hearing that no sight
Can glimpse or grasp on earth; to know a worth
In sound that can be found to touch and bless:
This is to know again a little mirth,
And to feel yet a hidden hand caress.
O Master, Thou hast wiped a big, big tear
Made of uncaptured yesterdays, and this
Strange message of a heat felt even here
In limbs o'er which prayer moved, bears grains of bliss
From where Thou art to where I am alone
With bits of light that have a law their own.

Strange message: News of the healing came last night.

WONDER UPON WONDER

We live upon the dance of molecules
That turn and turn all burning on a wave
Of patterned thought, and yet some little jew'ls
Of patterns unobserved would at times crave
To be let loose from Order duly bound
By distances well marked 'tween world and world,
And Thou, 'twould seem, this night hast some sport found
In toying with such forces hither hurled.
Can this be true, O King, O Queen, this thing
Divulged when all was o'er and sensed to be
Too stunning for a whim and known to ring
Of essences unknown that none should see?
That Mother and that Son should be perceived –
This is a pattern cosmic rays have weaved.

                                        6/12
                            (during the all-night vigil
                                for the Immaculate)

SEVEN YEARS

What days have passed since last I trod herein,
And heard the sound of silence 'tween these walls!
What store of moments since has entered in
To Memory's deep banks, whose chasm calls
Throughout all time within the soul that holds
For aye and aye the marks traced in the mind
That must live on and on, for that the folds
Of Thought leave not the soul of human kind.
It was upon a day, upon an hour
That many hours slipped by and many more
Came in from galaxies whose unknown pow'r
Ope'd regions dark and light, for by the door
Of this small massive house the pressing weight
Of years withheld was held by poisèd Fate.

9/12
(in retreat,
Roscrea)

THE SOUND OF VESPERS

We do refuse at times a precious thing
With eyes askance and looking far away
At what may never come, and blessings cling
Not long unto the heart that will not stay
And wait their gentle coming. We are one
When we are all in wanting, but want oft
Too many wanted things beneath the sun
And fail to look ahead or gaze aloft.
To think, this beauty was within my grasp
And waited but a nod of heart and will,
That this small hand ne'er e'er again shall clasp
The cowl that wraps the soul in whiteness still –
This is a pain that hurts where it can hurt,
For 'twas lost in an hour scarce all alert.

9/12
(Roscrea)

Ask Jesus...

O Master, hid beneath the sacred veil,
Unheard, unseen by them that walk this way
Of wanderings oft thought of no avail,
Thou hast yet found a voice upon this day,
And this same pen that writes was held by one
Who heard th'unheard of earth, for Thou didst steer
The etchings of a life, and Priest and Nun
Were uttered and thus made by scribblings here.
'Twould seem that these my friends were made for Thee,
And that Thou'dst have my tongue not vowed to die
But to bear sounds of silenced Verity
To ears of hungr'ing lambs that for it cry;
That in a day or two the æons moved
This nib o'er crooked lines by Wisdom grooved.

1/1/93

STUDENT
(among the Jesuits)

Along the corridors of learning here
We walk again, and gain a little more
For thought and mutterance, for very near
To those who pick the sleeping brains of yore
Are hov'ring weighty truths, and we are one
With souls that have long gone – gone on and on
To knowings deepened much, for such have done
Their thinking – for each thought for one day shone.
O Thinker of the world, to know and rest
Within Thine ancient vision, and to hear
These syllables traced, steered at Thy behest,
This is to know that this vast aisle is clear,
And that the Hand that holds me holds it all
And bids me but walk on where angels call.

These syllables here traced: the messages given through a little child.

STENCH

The meaning of an æon in a word
Too short for what it holds, for HELL holds all
The words and sounds of anguish ever heard
And ever to be heard till stars shall fall
From their long wand'rings in the firmament –
This means too much for one, who knows too well
The merit of entrancèd merriment
In opening the jaws of this dark dell.
That thou, foul Fiend and father of the Lie,
Shouldst deign to scowl and stir at this small page,
And cut across the currents wherein cry
The fragments of a soul that wails the age
It wasted for all time, means but one thing:
Some utterness of utt'rance here doth cling.

Hell: The Hell Manuscript, translated from the French, was being published by friends in the North.
Currents: For no reason, everything inexplicably behaved strengely during the operations preparatory to its printing.

WAYFARER

From day to day they come and ring again
And leave a blessing for a little food,
And though the sponge of mem'ry little gain
Of well-held facts in Study's high-strung mood,
To know that there is warmth within the hand
And heart that opens wide and passes on
A morsel from the table whereon stand
The mercies that feed all that here have gone;
To know, I say, that eyes see in our eyes
The glitter of a smile where there has been
Much pointed looking – 'tis to tap the sighs
Of many worlds of sorrow that unseen
Turn on an axis hid, 'fraid of the cold,
And carrying a load that ne'er was told.

14/2
(St Valentine)

O God, come to our aid...
(Ynys Cwyfan)

I little thought that I would walk again
Upon this corner of the world, our own,
And rest upon this wooden bench so plain
That held a double weight before, as stone
On ancient sacred stone heard echo well
The lullaby of prayer that rocked a load
Of loving trust, nor could I e'er foretell
That, not apart, but here in our abode
We would rewalk an hour that had walked by,
And hallow its rich seconds, not with this
Fond madness that but made us deeply cry
In our sharp sev'ring, but, nay, with a kiss
Made of a Vesper song in harmony
That was wed in a quiet memory.

CANCER

There is a word that halts all utterance
And dampens every echo but its own.
There is a silence that bids moments, once
So happy in their flow, think of th'unknown
And tap at its vast regions. There is here
Within the face that smiled a heavy cloud
Of possible farewells, for to be near
Is well, save when thy nearest wears a shroud.
O little being made for suffering,
On Carmel's Mount, thou didst find Calvary,
And 'twould seem that the Crucified would bring
Thy feet to one last nail ere thou be free
To suffer and to die, for 'tis not ours,
But His to shape the edges of our hours.

TRIDENTINE MASS

We have been hasty to leap o'er the years
That fashioned our own being, we have been
All Mind, that could not shed e'en little tears
For what we'd see no more – for the unseen
Of Mystery hath hurt this morn my eyes
With weepings of past days, with hours gone by
With neither haste nor hurry 'neath the skies
Of yesterday and yesterday's dim cry.
I heard within the cloud that covered us
In burning wings the things that will not go
As quickly as we think, and list'ning thus
I heard the yearns of some who once did know
The pull of ancient grace, the face of God,
The tremor that bid man here step unshod.

Beth ydyw hyn a elwir, dyner un,
Yn gariad gennyt ti? Beth ydyw hyn
Y'th wnaed ohono? Beth, fwyn, addfwyn fun,
Yw'r deunydd crai, pa foleciwlau prin
Yw sylfaen hyn o ansawdd? O gorff gwan,
Na fedr ond rhoi, rhoi ac eto rhoi,
Nes rhoddi d'einioes oll i'r unig fan
A welodd wawr dy wyneb a fu ddoe
Ac echdoe a phob echdoe fel yn awr
Yn gwenu ar y boen yng nghreithiau'r dydd –
Deg gorffyn mân, dy galon anferth fawr
Yfory ac yfory'n curo fydd
Pan fydd y rhai a geraist wedi mynd,
A thithau'n dal heb 'nabod calon ffrind.

MONGOLOID

A hand is but a little, little thing,
Too small to hold the all of human kind
Here where it moves, for what here moves doth bring
The particles of being hid behind
The epiderm of man; doth bring a thought,
A soul that travels in a molecule,
Across the tiny touching cells all fraught
With heat of meaning taught in ne'er a school.
O little child of accidental fault,
Deep in thy distant prison, where no man
May walk or hear thee think, one sound can halt
The sounds that pass thee by, though softer than
The amplitude of skill, for skill is none
Within the tingle of a little one.

The epiderm...: During the whole time of prayer she insisted on
holding my hand.

THE FIRING SQUAD
(at which Fr Tony, a fellow-student,
gave absolution to the innocent)

There are but bullets 'tween a living soul
And what it heard and shifted, what it sensed
As its accustomed home, and but a hole
Or two or three let fly a cry condensed
With all the pain of parting, for the scream
That settles in the sky asunder racks
The wriggles of a being that did seem
All one ere came these little chinks and cracks.
A bullet walks but once, and onward goes
The naked roving of the spectred mind
With weight of mem'ry laden, 'mid the throes
Of many hurting moments left behind.
And there are many hovering around,
Still hearing but a distant sharp, sharp sound.

FOOTBALL
(St Patrick's Day)

For all the world to move around a ball
So small, so round, so bound by frenzied ire
Of bounds unknown; for one white spot to call
The eyeballs of a populace entire
From sockets startled, rolled all into one,
One sole absorbed direction – for all hope
Of bliss and misery to turn on none
But bouncèd fate, for which lands tug and grope –
This is the height of Earth's civility,
Where matters of great moment matter more
Than mutterings of uttered verity
Tossed in a world apart, 'neath some heart's door
Unknocked, unentered, yet kicked oft a time,
For none to this round planet stopped to climb.

Alcohol

There sparkles yet a demon in the wave
Of molecules undammed, and damnèd fumes
Traverse the coddled cells that softly rave
A little more as each loose lip consumes
The master of its speech, and as the night
Rolls into thicker dark, the spark of wit
That was in the first sip knows not its might,
Nor will the dawn recall what carried it.
O little glass so empty and so full
Of human kind, what verity so foul
Dost thou from unleashed entrails so well pull
That thou canst disembody e'en a soul,
And in a moment poured pour out a life
Into th'abyss where long wept Erin's wife?

                                          17/3
                                        (Dublin)

HOSPITAL

To weep is not for men when fully grown,
Unless it be for this, the all of man
Undone by sadness huge. O! thing unknown,
Foreseen not yesterday! O! image wan,
Pale shadow of what was! O! horror! No!
Can this event now be the all that is?
My father, my own father! Do I know
The one in this changed body that was his?
To cry, and not to stop; to cry, to cry
Is to be old a child. Yet 'tis the child
That looks, looks up, looks high as 'twould look high
Long, long ago at one faint smile so mild
That it beamed Home, my home, my only home;
And to what shattered homing have I come?

27/3

BACH

Will I behold again these pallid eyes
That once did twinkle at a loving ball
Of sleeping trust that they had bid arise
From nothingness and void? Will I hear call
The name that they bid be, by this frail voice
Again, or will the pain of hurting parts
Prolong the metal pow'r of this long choice
Wherein the ancient end of all things starts?
O little part of Man that works too well
When nought else moves, what mischief wilt thou wreak?
The Will is still the force that holds this knell
Alone, and by the hour. O! meanings, speak!
Let something reach the depth that kindled me,
And bid the flick'ring spark that lit me, be.

AGAIN

Much time has passed since last we said, "Farewell,
Sweet little one," at this same water's edge,
And held within our hand the soul that well
We knew, and now anew on this same ledge
I sit and write upon a passing pain
Made of a hurting bliss, for this is all
That comes again as we an hour regain
Of æons lost that from afar still call.
The passing of an hour holds many things
That will not pass again, and there are tears
Bedewing all the years that Chronos' wings
Tap happily along, for there are fears
That morrows will have sorrows yet untold,
And we do well upon a while to hold.

2/4
(Holyhead)

SHRINE

A weighted soul was ne'er a soul at rest,
Nor was there long a happiness within
The laden mind borne on the swollen crest
Of heightened joy unfrightened by the sin
Which bade it be, which urged it to be more,
More, more again, for pain of Conscience known
Could but be hid by this loud bidding's roar
Made of a wanting that did all else drown.
O! yet what lingers here? What mists of Dark
Here move, removed from blackened hours whose stench
Was sweetened 'twixt these walls? How oft the spark
Of Hell's ill judged delight did this scent quench?
O little place where Grace did find a space,
I love thee well, for I feel here His Face.

(Sitting in the Shrine of Divine Mercy,
Monday of Holy Week.)

279

DAD

Pa freuddwyd neu ba hunllef sydd fan hyn
O dan amrannau nad agorant mwy
At olau dydd, a pha edrychiad syn
Yw'r olwg wag ddi-olwg sydd yn hwy
Na noson unrhyw gwsg? Ai dyma'r un
A roddodd fod i mi, a'm daliodd gynt?
Ai dyma'r wyneb cu a adwaen? P'run?
P'un oedd yr awr newidiodd fyth ei hynt?
Fy nhad, fy nhyner graig, beth gipiodd di
O'n gofal ac o'n byd, cans er yn fyw
Nid bywyd mo dy wedd, a sain dy gri
Sydd bell o'r adlais hoff a lonnai'n clyw?
Fy nhad, fy annwyl dad, gwellhad ni fydd,
A'r bore hwn yw diwedd hen, hen dydd.

17/4
(Ysbyty Gwynedd)

WEDI MYND

Ffarwèl, anwylaf un, dos ar dy daith
I'r parthau pell, o ba le nad oes troi
Yn ôl i'r bröydd hyn. Rhy faith, rhy faith
Yw'r siwrnai olaf hon a ddaw i gloi
Ein teithio oll – rhy faith i'r meddwl gwan
Na fedr ddilyn mwy dy grwydro di,
O gymar oes, na weli eto fan
Yr oriau byrion hyn a rannwn ni.
Ffarwèl, fwyn ffrind; rhaid dychwel am a ddêl
O oriau nad ŷnt debyg yn eu llif
I'r rhai a rifwn ni, ac yno gwêl
Â'r llygaid hyn a gaeaist, beth yw rhif
Yr oesoedd sydd o'n blaen, cans tawel iawn
Yr awr a leddfodd uffern un prynhawn.

17/4

IT HURTS
(Dad's last sentence)

This is the road o'er which no man returns,
The lonely mile where voyagers have none
To guide or point the way, for here each learns
The ancient learning in this moment won
By all who reached its rim, and this long sleep
That in a breath undrawn begins to be
Into an unmarked cosmos doth now peep
Beneath these fastened eyes that all things see.
Farewell, sweet face of care, that held the world
In safety while all rocked; farewell, sweet gaze
That shall not see again or hear a word
From these receding shores of passing days.
For though we may love well, 'tis well to know
That we must hurt a little as we go.

TEARS

(Funeral)

To know that there is music in the dark
To which we send thee on, good kindest friend,
And that e'en little beauties bear a mark
Of order that some harmony doth send
From very far away – to know that we
Move from a land of song to Song's long home
And travel to where singing can but be
Tapped onward by the æons' metronome –
This is to know, know well, behind a tear
That there is in a casket yet a shade
Of kindliness asmile with something near
To what our many masters have not made.
For I can hear my father in this song,
And there moves o'er these rafters some strange throng.

HWYLIO

Ffarwèl, fy Nghymru, dir atgofion mwyn
Y dyddiau fu!
Ffarwèl, fy mebyd, na ddaw eto'i swyn
Na'i seiniau cu
Yn ôl dros donnau'r amser sydd ar ddod
Dros orwel pell
Cyfandir estron rod.

Ffarwèl, dir hiraeth, bro yr annwyl drem
Na ddaw yn ôl,
A chwithau, oriau pur magwraeth lem
Y dyner gôl.
Nid oes a erys bellach ond y rhain,
Y pethau bach
Rhy fawr i'r olaf maen.

Ffarwèl, y Wlad a hoffais, ac a fydd
Y fwynaf oll.
Ffarwèl, hen erwau'r hen funudau cudd
Sy'n awr yngholl
Yn nyfnder hyn o eigion ddaeth i'n troi
O'r deigryn gwan
Sydd ynom yn crynhoi.

Yfory fe fydd rheswm am a fu,
Ac fe fydd dydd
Y gwelwn eto'r pethau bychain cu
Yn bethau sydd
Yn rhan o'r hyn a'n gwnaeth, yn rhan o'n taith
O lan i lan
Y gwir a'r pur hoff baith.

25/4
(Tôn: Lux benigna)

LLYTHYR

Yr hyn a erys ar fodfeddi prin
Papuryn brau, helaethach yw na'r byd
Sy'n troi a throi'n ei flaen drwy'r oesoedd hyn
Nad oedant am un dyn, a rhyfedd ddrud
Y rhad ddi-raid ronynnau o rwy bren
A falwyd rywdro rywsut gan ryw law
Na wyddai am a ddaliai'r ddalen wen
O'r ddoe i'r heddiw ac i'r 'fory ddaw.
O anweledig un, na theimlaf i
Ond yn nirgrynu tawel hyn o sain
Di-sŵn d'addfwynaf gyffyrddiadau di,
Aroglau d'enaid sy' dan amlen fain.
Ac y mae mewn llinellau glas ryw swyn
A fedr eto ystyr Ystyr ddwyn.

28/5

Rain

When there is darkness in a summer's day
And coldness in the soul that was not warmed
By touch of words or sound of loving play
For many morns and nights; when there have formed
Clouds of unknowing o'er horizons vast
And pockets of an absence in the air
That we not always knew, and when at last
The distant fairness 'gins to be too fair,
Then is there but a language made of sighs
That none shall ever hear, for fear withholds
The text of verity from strangers' eyes,
And neighbours see not well what love beholds.
For we are only what we are alone,
And loneliness knows well, knows well its own.

PRIESTHOOD

To be all Thine, my God, to be all Thine,
And to stand where the feet of Thine have stood
Since Christendom with ancient wording fine
First set apart the race that hath withstood
The turnings of a world – to hold the Hand
That holds the all of all: 'twould be the blest
And hallowed holding of empow'red Command
That ne'er an angel held at his behest.
'Twould be, my Lord, a little thing for Thee
To whisper for a whisper, for herein,
Within a little nod, rocks all to be
Or not to be set loose by one sound's din –
Yet, yet I know that were I giv'n a word,
A melody of Mercy could be heard.

LETTER

And is there truth in this, that but a child
Heard the unheard and knew what was not known
To heads full-crammed? Is't thus the æons smiled
At our intense forethinking, and was shown,
Not with a vision but a syllable
Tapped on a clear heart's ear, Tomorrow's form?
And did I too brush off th'unknowable
As but a drifting cloud of Chronos' storm?
O Wisdom wise as Time, and older still,
Dost Thou behold the causes causing all
That can be caused to be, and can a Will
As patient as the day bid evening fall
Where it was meant to fall, on happenings
Long wrought, long fraught with heavy little things?

Lough Derg

To feel the moments passing, one by one,
And nurse the seconds of an ancient pain;
To have a while to halt tomorrow's sun,
Lest it too quickly come; nay, to regain
The sparkle of a yesterday long gone,
And to be shriven, head to frozen toe –
This is to have vast nothings full well done
And gaze upon a comma as we go.
The nothing of a muttering as long
As these strange Celtic patterns hewn by hands
Worn by an unknown soul, a mist-blown throng,
That, aiming all at Wasting, conquered lands
That shall not fade away – the naught of all
Is poised upon an islet e'er so small.

PURDAN

Mae yna fannau bychain hynod fawr,
Llecynnau lle nad ydyw lle yn bod,
Ac y mae oriau na fesurant awr,
Eiliadau nad ŷnt dan gynefin rod.
Nid oes I boen gyfnewid, nid oes ddydd
Na hanes rhwng dwy oes: y loes a ddaeth
A ddaw yn ôl drwy'r gwyntoedd heddiw sydd
Yn uno cyfandiroedd ar un traeth.
O randir mwyn, yn dwyn yr atgo'n ôl
O wynfyd ein ffolineb, beth yw hyn,
Y rhyfedd faith Ddoethineb ganwaith ffôl
Sy'n denu enctid gwlad at 'stumiau syn
A wnaed gan hen ieuenctid dynol ryw
Na wyddai ddim am ddim ond diwedd byw?

6/7
(Lough Derg)

HOUSE OF PRAYER
(Feast of St Benedict)

Was it perchance for this that Thou didst call
And call and call again across the seas
That bore me back through happ'nings hid and small
To where Thy work begins? Thine eye that sees
Tomorrow's shapeless form ere it be named,
Does it now gaze and lovingly behold
This wending of a way by Thy hand claimed,
This spending of a soul to Thee enfold?
Domus orationis – this old sound
Was heard before, and on this very day,
By cloisterers that ancient Peace had found
In turning to Obscurity away.
And there is company upon an isle
Where wingèd brethren have been known to smile.

THIRST

Oh! for the beauty of a mystic rite
Of ancient trappings weaved, of motions made
That in a clouded distance hide the Light
Of uncreated Presence deftly weighed
On little flutt'ring wings of glory bound
To circle and adore – adore, adore...
Adore! The sound ill fits the thinking found
In tomes of heavy Intellect's tense store.
There is no fairness in a lengthy word
As in a ray of Tabor; there is none
In all the functions where there hath not stirred
A little leap of feeling let to run...
And there is hunger in a hungry world
For something out of hackneyed orbit hurled.

LEAD, KINDLY LIGHT

When knowledge there is not of what shall be
And certainty evades the peering eye,
When morrows hang unclad, and all we see
Is trouble in a very troubled sky,
Then there is but a song, a little plaint
That bore a heart's full weight at this same spot
Before at oft a pain – nay, two hearts faint
Once cast upon this strain their common lot.
O master of the pen, hold out thy hand
And lead this lost, stray child – lead, lead me on
To where thy two great feet were led to stand
Upon that Will wherein alone light shone.
For I know not the way, and can but take
A little step, lest I some huge plunge make.

ANGEL OF IRELAND

O little one as great as this great land
O'er which thy wings are spread,
Stretch forth at this dark hour this shining hand
That has through ages led
The sorrows of our past, and at the last
And darkest moment of our foe
Shine in our night,
And Darkness overthrow.

O hidden one as fair as this fair isle
Where greater things have been
In other days long gone, shine on awhile
This dusk, for we have seen
A little of the morrow that may be
Our own, our own perhaps again
Through thee, good friend,
If we thy friendship gain.

O! little stranger, strangely known to us
Through rays that pass us by,
For we think not to linger sometimes thus
To gaze into the sky
Where angel faces have their places hid
And long at length in bliss to beam
Upon a land
That bears an ancient gleam.

(On melody specially composed)

SHAKEN

O gentle Mother, thou didst have a word,
A mighty word for me – a word that means
More than the many mutterings long heard
And bearing matter scarce: a word where leans
The Mother of my Master unto me
And says enough to show that there is more,
More caring and more knowing hid in thee,
Sweet Mary, than I ever thought before.
I love thee, little Woman, mighty Queen,
And press thee, though I see thee not, for now
The knowledge that these tender hands unseen
Enfold me in this way and know well how
To steer the blind, as long as he is blind,
Means that at last I can leave thought behind.

DOUBLY SHAKEN
(by a call from Ireland)

There are in wires small particles of mind
That with but little shifting bid it move
The all of what we are, and we can find
In e'en a handed message moving love
And linger in a warmth of being known
And wanted upon earth – but words from Heav'n
Till recently came not 'neath this old tone,
Nor were these lines to angel peeps oft giv'n.
To think, high Friend, that thou didst deign to smile
Especially for me, and want to say
A word to mortal man, and think awhile
How best to have it said – this is to play
A game with mystic friends I never knew,
And to be rocked by shocks of glory's hue.

Wires: My Mother, at home in Wales, took the totally
unexpected call: the Angel and Our Lady liked the hymn.

DETAILS
(given last week about the future)

There is a jig-saw in the hand of God,
And pieces have their place, yet I thought not
As I from this small bedroom shyly trod
Forth to another world, that my strange lot
Was eyed and measured with such ancient skill –
Scarce did I hope, or dream that this could be:
That all the pond'rings of th'Eternal Will
Should through a child's heart's ear be giv'n to me.
To know, my Lord, that there is Order there
And that a lonely star beams on its way
Alone, yet not alone, and only where
'Twas coaxed to shine for its short little day –
This is to rest upon a mighty Hand
And on a crumbling æon safe to stand.

This small bedroom: Written at home in Wales.

PICTURES

To know that thou art gone, my father, gone
Into a realm unknown, that nevermore
Will this familiar gaze, that briefly shone
Upon this clever eye, beam as before
Into the magic square that holds a day
Suspended for all others, and to know
That home means not all home and that to say
The oldest word of all calls no one now:
This is to hold an absence in the hand,
And on the page to see the age that was
Unhurried in its march; yet there to stand
Framed in a halvèd instant even as
All others pass away – this little thing
Is giv'n to men with which to hours to cling.

1/8
(Wales)

Anamchára

The heart hath oft a secret, and there lie
'Neath every breast hid continents of thought,
And there walk many beings that no eye
Surveyed or met, for that none ever sought
To walk into this land, and I have known
The frigid smiles of many who smile not
From soul to soul, from depth to depth all shown,
And there are that for Grace have grace forgot.
'Tis strange that we be called to love not here
With all the love of Man, and yet that we
In knowing but one knowing be so near
A seeing of what eye did never see.
For I perceive abroad some rays that peep
Into a corner that but one did keep.

1/8
(Wales)